THEODORE THE GREAT

THEO DORE

the

GREAT

~

CONSERVATIVE CRUSADER

~

DANIEL RUDDY

**REGNERY
HISTORY**

Regnery History™ is a trademark of Salem Communications Holding Corporation; Regnery® is a registered trademark of Salem Communications Holding Corporation

Library of Congress Cataloging-in-Publication Data

Ruddy, Daniel, author.
  Theodore the great : conservative crusader / Daniel Ruddy.
    pages cm
  ISBN 978-1-62157-264-0
  1. Roosevelt, Theodore, 1858-1919. 2. Presidents--United States--Biography. 3. United States--Politics and government--1901-1909. I. Title.
  E757.R937 2015
  973.91'1092--dc23
  [B]
                                        2015029442

Published in the United States by
Regnery History
An imprint of Regnery Publishing
A Division of Salem Media Group
300 New Jersey Ave NW
Washington, DC 20001
www.RegneryHistory.com

Manufactured in the United States of America

10 9 8 7 6 5 4 3 2 1

Books are available in quantity for promotional or premium use. For information on discounts and terms, please visit our website: www.Regnery.com.

Distributed to the trade by
Perseus Distribution
250 West 57th Street
New York, NY 10107

To Little Wing

CONTENTS

~

PART IV: TR AS PRESIDENT: FOREIGN POLICY

PART V: ASSESSING HIS TWO TERMS

As President, Mr. Roosevelt could speak progressively and act conservatively. But as a private citizen, what has he but words to rely upon?[1]
—*London Times* editorial after TR's speech at Osawatomie, Kansas, raised fears that the ex-president had become a socialist

It is well to keep in mind the remark of Frederick the Great that if he wished to punish a province he would allow it to be governed by philosophers.[2]
—TR expressing his belief that practical realists made much better rulers than ideological doctrinaires

When we shake hands, we shake the world.[3]
—Inscription of the German leader, Kaiser Wilhelm II, to TR on a photograph of the two men at their first face-to-face meeting in 1910

INTRODUCTION

~

When Theodore Roosevelt died in January 1919, his staunch-est friend, Henry Cabot Lodge, cried out in the U.S. Senate, "Greatheart is gone!"[4] To Lodge, and to countless other Americans, Roosevelt had seemed like a romantic hero, almost from the moment he burst onto the public stage.

A decade before Roosevelt reached the White House, the sitting president, Grover Cleveland, prophesized: "You do not know Theodore Roosevelt. I do, and I tell you that he is one of the ablest politicians either party ever had and the ablest Republican politician in this generation. The country will find this out in time."[5] The then–Speaker of the House of Representatives, Thomas Reed, was equally sure Roosevelt was des-tined for greatness. "We've got an American of blood and iron—a com-ing man," he told a new member of Congress. "You want to watch this man, for he is a new world Bismarck and Cromwell combined, and you will see him President yet."[6] That was how Roosevelt, a man in his early thirties, was viewed by the most powerful men in the U.S. government.

The comparisons with Bismarck and Cromwell were apt. Like Bismarck, Roosevelt wanted his country to be feared, respected, and united. Like Cromwell, he approached politics with a passionate, even religious fervor. Roosevelt wrote a biography of Cromwell and saw himself cast from a Cromwellian mold, a "General of the Lord with his Bible and Sword,"[7] a sword Roosevelt intended to wield against the selfish plutocracy and corrupt "machine politics" of the Gilded Age.

One of Roosevelt's British friends, Lord Morley, had a different take on the twenty-sixth president, but he also described TR in religious terms, believing he was "an interesting combination of St. Vitus and St. Paul."[8] He saw Roosevelt not as a Cromwellian warrior but as a flamboyant entertainer fueled by endless reserves of nervous energy (St. Vitus is the patron saint of actors and epileptics). And instead of a Bismarckian strongman, he saw his friend as a political evangelist who used his extraordinary talents to persuade rather than to intimidate.

While astute observers saw the seeds of greatness in Roosevelt many years before he reached the White House, others saw a quick-tempered, impetuous, and potentially dangerous man who could not be trusted to wield presidential power. He never shook off this reputation for rash behavior, but he did, as we'll see, turn it to his advantage, especially in foreign affairs.

NOT A LIBERAL PROGRESSIVE

Bizarrely, "progressives," as American liberals are now often called, have tried to adopt Theodore Roosevelt as one of their own, just as many conservatives have tried to disown him. But this is to get Roosevelt exactly backwards.

At his core, Roosevelt was a conservative who used progressive language to inspire a spirit of nationalism in the American people. Unlike many modern progressives, he had not a smidgen of ambivalence about American power or his country's exceptional place in the world. He was a patriot who did not see American history as a litany of sins. And while he believed in the power of government to do good, as did his fellow conservative Alexander Hamilton, he was not, unlike many modern progressives, a man who saw merit in socialism. In fact, he denounced socialism as an unjust scheme that would damage the United States if it were ever implemented, declaring, "Jacobinism, socialism, communism, nihilism and anarchism—these are the real foes of a democratic republic."[9] On another occasion, he said, "The most cruel form of injustice that can be devised would be to give a man who has not earned it the reward that ought to come only to the man who has earned it."[10] Or again:

> The Roman mob, living on the bread given them by the State and clamoring for excitement and amusement to be purveyed by the State, represent for all time the very nadir to which a free and self-respecting population of workers can sink if they grow habitually to rely upon others, and especially upon the State, either to furnish them charity, or to permit them to plunder, as a means of a livelihood.[11]

Roosevelt was, in fact, a fiscal conservative, who believed that Congress had to live within its budget. Even when he asked for the expansion of the United States Navy, he wanted the money to come from revenue surpluses rather than borrowing.

He opposed the income tax until it became a *fait accompli* with Congress's approval of the sixteenth amendment to the Constitution in 1910. He kept the currency stable by adopting an inflexible "sound money" policy based on the gold standard (like J. P. Morgan and Ronald Reagan, he favored a "strong dollar" to prevent inflation).

A sensible and cautious man in confronting politically charged issues, he supported the continuation of policies that had produced prosperity throughout his generation, including a high tariff wall to protect American industry and agriculture from foreign competition. The importance of Big Business in generating prosperity did not escape him, and his celebrated "Trust Busting" was carried out with laser-beam precision in order to encourage competition without disrupting the nation's economy. TR's conservative economic policies, which largely continued those of Wall Street's favorite son, William McKinley, were validated by national prosperity throughout his presidency.

He was also a social conservative. The father of six celebrated family life and vehemently opposed abortion, birth control, and divorce. A law-and-order governor and former police commissioner, he strongly supported the death penalty and wanted it imposed on rapists. A lifelong hunter, he owned many firearms and carried a concealed revolver when he was president. On national security, he was a hawk before the term became a cliché, willing to use military force to protect American interests.

When Roosevelt used the word *progressive*, it was in the same way that Edmund Burke, the intellectual founder of modern conservatism, used the word *reform*—as the lifeblood of an active conservatism that could prevent social discontent and revolution. Roosevelt was a conservative crusader who believed in a strong, united America. Progressivism, as he understood it, was the means to achieve that end. In June 1918, six months before his death, he succinctly defined his conservatism this way:

> There must be sincere purpose to push forward and remedy wrong, but there must likewise be firm refusal to submit either to the leadership of the criminal fringe or the lunatic fringe. Class hatred is a mighty poor substitute for American brotherhood. If we are wise we will proceed by evolution and not revolution. But Bourbon refusal to move forward at all merely invites revolution.[12]

PART I

THE FIRST

MODERN

PRESIDENT

~

CHAPTER ONE

TR'S ROLLER-COASTER REPUTATION

~

Theodore Roosevelt was always controversial, but he was also enormously popular. In late 1907, fifty-five newspapers around the country asked whether President Roosevelt, then completing his second term, should run for a third. Of the 21,475 people who responded, 69 percent said yes.[1] This was an astounding level of approval on its own merits, never mind that it rose up against the long held presidential tradition established by George Washington of retiring after two terms.

To the astonishment of his critics, who repeatedly called him a dictator, Roosevelt had pledged after his election victory in 1904 not to seek a third term. That third term was his for the taking in 1908, and, while it is rash to indulge in counterfactual history, given the unity of the Republican Party under his leadership, it is easy to imagine his earning a fourth and a fifth term as well. At the end of five terms, he would have been only sixty-two—eight years younger than Ronald Reagan was when he began his presidency.

Roosevelt's immense popularity is apparent in the results of another newspaper survey, this one conducted by the *Baltimore Sun* in February 1909. The paper asked readers, "What will Theodore Roosevelt's nickname be in the history books of the future?"[2] The survey results, whatever their limits, show a departing president regarded with affection (Teddy, Teddy Bear), respect (Theodore the Great, the Big Stick, the Strenuous President, the Trust Buster), and admiration (the Peacemaker, Father of the Panama Canal, the Rough Rider).

Most Popular Nicknames in 1909	Number of Responses
Teddy	69
The Big Stick	66
The Strenuous President	59
The Trust Buster	58
The Peacemaker	54
The Rough Rider	47
The Teddy Bear	38
Father of the Panama Canal	38
The Simple Speller[3]	35
Theodore the Great	30

It seems fair to say that no American president has left the White House more liked by the public than Theodore Roosevelt, but not all responses to the *Sun*'s question were complimentary. A vocal minority of Americans saw him as an autocrat who usurped the constitutional powers of the legislative and judicial branches and as a reckless imperialist who shamelessly flouted the sovereignty of weak nations in Latin America. Members of this faction suggested the following nicknames:

Theodore Caesar	The Revised Constitution
The Egoist	The American Sovereign Pontiff
Theodore Maximus	The Biggest "I" On Earth
The Infallible	The One Who Knew It All
The Congressional Whip	Ipse Dixit* Teddy
The Modern Nimrod	The Supreme Judge
The Exaggerated Ego	The Modern Alexander
Veni, Vedi, Vici	The Dictator
My Policies	The American Demigod
Almost a Nero	The Bad Dream

(*Ipse Dixit is a Latin phrase meaning "He said it himself." It is used to describe authoritative statements made without proof.)

While Roosevelt's critics often accused him of being a vainglorious potentate, less serious detractors ridiculed his ungainly physical appearance (Him with the Teeth, the Gargoyle in the White House); mocked him as a sort of P. T. Barnum with a childlike need to be the center of attention (Too Much Teddy, the Greatest Show on Earth, Theodore the Preposterous, the Limelight, Mr. Bunk, the King of Capers, Teddy the Tiresome, the Blarney Stone, the Airship that Never Came Down); or pushed back against his political moralizing (the Political Evangelist, the Common Scold, the Dragon of Right, the High Priest of Good Morals).

Other nicknames suggested by the readers of the Baltimore Sun include: the Lion Hunter, the Superman, the Busy-Body, the Chief Detective of the United States, the Observed Observer, the Hero of San Juan Hill, the Gladiator, Theodore the Little, the Nightmare of Grafters, the Agitator, the Prince of Discord, the Archangel, the Ruthless, the Preacher, the Encyclopedia, Panama Teddy, Theodore the Impossible, the Man that Scared John D. [Rockefeller], Seven Long Years!, the Monitor of All Creation, the Lone Truth-Teller, the Promoter of Panics, the Hero Told to Oversee (anagram of Theodore Roosevelt), Roosevelt the Mighty, the

Jack of All Trades, the Oracle of Oyster Bay, the Janus of America, and Xantippe (the overbearing wife of Socrates).

To most of the country, though, he was simply "Teddy"—not a father-figure like George Washington but a respected big brother. No other American president except "Abe" Lincoln has been honored in this way. Roosevelt did not insist that Americans call him "Teddy," the way President Carter insisted that everyone call him "Jimmy." He preferred, in fact, to be called Theodore. But he appreciated, however reluctantly, the moniker verdict of the people, who on the whole thought of him as a beloved family member, not an aloof politician.

BURNISHING HIMSELF AS THE ROUGH RIDER

Roosevelt expected to be remembered as Theodore the Great—an honorific that paid tribute to his ambition, his energy, and his achievements. An aristocrat with a privileged upbringing, his image among the American people was, paradoxically, one of a rough-riding frontiersman who had been a cowboy and hunter in the untamed West, who, when he turned to politics, was a tribune of the people leading a high-minded crusade against government corruption in the cultured East.

The defining characteristic of Roosevelt's personality was his need to show the world he was manly and strong. In this respect, he was nothing like Abraham Lincoln, whose iron will to win and steely, inscrutable resolve were kept hidden beneath an affable and folksy persona, or George Washington, whose tightly controlled temper rarely exploded around others. He wasn't like Thomas Jefferson, infamous for his preference for intrigue over frontal assaults on political enemies, or even the choleric Andrew Jackson, who let his Indian-killer, "Sharp Knife" reputation speak for itself.

Among American statesmen, Roosevelt most resembles Alexander Hamilton. Both were relatively small in stature, yearned for battlefield glory, and were aggressive in their defense of their honor. Roosevelt, of course, had to build his body up, to compensate for the ravages of his childhood asthma. Hamilton built up his mind as an aggressive autodidact and was an eager young militiaman at the start of the Revolutionary War. Both Hamilton and Roosevelt achieved their lifelong desire for heroic combat in spectacular charges that ended wars, Hamilton leading the climactic assault at Yorktown in 1781 and Roosevelt leading the final assault on the Spanish entrenchments on Kettle Hill in Cuba in 1898. Both men were hawks who denounced dithering presidents (in Hamilton's case, John Adams; in TR's, William McKinley) for vacillating leadership as war loomed with a foreign foe (France in 1798, Spain in 1898). Both men possessed a soaring ambition for personal and national greatness, and a fearless personality that invited conflict with antagonists.

Before the Spanish-American War gave him the opportunity for military combat, Roosevelt settled for political combat. As a politician, he portrayed himself as a crusader against sinister forces, while showing himself as an heroic version of a common man, too, through stories he wrote for popular magazines that described his rough-and-tough life in the unforgiving Dakota Territory. On his arrival in the West, Roosevelt had at first been regarded as a soft, pampered "New York dude, who was all teeth and eyeglasses" but had quickly changed that reputation by breaking "the buckiest, ugliest cow ponies he could find,"[4] driving a corrupt sheriff out of town, tracking down and capturing horse thieves, and riding endless hours during the roundup with the rest of the hired hands. All this helped make Roosevelt an immensely popular politician.

POST-PRESIDENTIAL DIVE

But he made mistakes, too, which have harmed his reputation. His ill-advised decision in 1912 to bolt from the Republican Party and run for president as a Bull Moose Progressive made him seem power-hungry and erratic. The victory of Woodrow Wilson that year ended Roosevelt's political winning streak, which had begun in 1881 with his election to the New York Assembly at the age of twenty-three. His reputation did not recover during his seven remaining years of life.

When the *Lusitania*, a British ocean liner carrying 128 American civilians, was sunk by a German U-boat in 1915, Roosevelt insisted the United States, as a matter of national honor, join the war against Germany. Few, however, shared his view. Most Americans wanted to stay out of a horrific war in a distant land that did not seem to concern the United States. Refusing to flow with the popular pacific tide, he denounced Wilson for cultivating national apathy, but his pro-war agitation only decreased his popularity in a country that wanted to remain isolated from the world's troubles.

The loveable Teddy Bear was now viewed as recklessly belligerent, indifferent to the carnage that awaited America's youth in the trenches of France. "I think the American people feel a little tired of me,"[5] said a frustrated Roosevelt. He was defying public opinion as he had never dared to do while in the White House:

> I have spoken out as strongly and as clearly as possible, and I do not think it has had any effect beyond making people think that I am a truculent and bloodthirsty person, endeavoring futilely to thwart able, dignified, humane Mr. Wilson in his noble plan to bring peace everywhere by excellently written letters sent to persons who care nothing whatever for any letter that is not backed up by force![6]

Roosevelt's faded reputation did not benefit from his death in 1919. Warren Harding's "Return to Normalcy" campaign the following year rang the death knell of the progressive era and set the tone for the 1920s. Sickened by the carnage of World War I and eager for a quiet life, the American people embraced the enigmatic "Silent Cal" Coolidge—the antithesis of the preachy, crusading Roosevelt.

The Great Depression revived the spirit of reform that Roosevelt had fostered, and his reputation revived with it. His progressive-minded cousin Franklin Roosevelt found the clan's surname a political asset, and the title of his economic program, the New Deal, paid homage to TR's Square Deal. Leading the Democratic Party, FDR successfully positioned himself as a conservative reformer, just as TR had done a generation before, thwarting the attempt of TR's son, Ted Jr., to do the same within the Republican Party.

TR's reputation benefited from this cross-party endorsement of his legacy, but was hit with a powerful countervailing force when many liberal academics in the 1930s linked TR to the rise of European totalitarianism. It seemed to be a natural outgrowth of his militaristic, strongman style of leadership. Arthur Schlesinger Jr., for example, recalled the popular sentiment: "When I went to college in the 1930s, I was taught that Theodore Roosevelt was a blustering bully."[7] The first full-length biography of Theodore Roosevelt, Henry Pringle's Pulitzer Prize–winning volume published in 1931, added to this ugly, unfair picture by depicting his subject as a sham reformer whose remedies were at best superficial. Pringle, a cheerleader for Al Smith, the Democratic governor of New York, dismissed the Republican Roosevelt as a "magnificent child"[8] and "violently adolescent person"[9] who was "merely a strutting personification of an America newly powerful in a new century, but not quite grown up and hence dangerous."[10]

THE VIEW FROM MOUNT RUSHMORE

If TR's reputation was suffering among the intellectual class, he remained a popular figure—popular enough for sculptor Gutzon Borglum to chisel Roosevelt's face, along with those of Washington, Jefferson, and Lincoln, on Mount Rushmore in South Dakota between 1934 and 1939. Borglum had admired Roosevelt, having worked for him during the 1912 Bull Moose presidential campaign. Had another sculptor designed the monument, Andrew Jackson's might have been the fourth face, or three presidents might have been depicted rather than four.

Roosevelt's apotheosis on Mount Rushmore might have had less to do with his politics, though, than with his firm place as an American character. In the popular Cary Grant film *Arsenic and Old Lace* (1944), two kindly spinsters poison lonely old men and dispose of their corpses with the help of their crazy brother, Teddy, who believes himself to be Theodore Roosevelt. When not screaming "Charge!" and running up the stairs to San Juan Hill (the second floor of the house), Teddy is happy to bury the murdered men in the basement, convinced they were unfortunate victims of "yellow fever" contracted while digging the Panama Canal.

The film, a dark comedy, helped revive the image of old, loveable "Teddy," but it also reinforced the erroneous idea that he was a touched-in-the-head cowboy adventurer, an avuncular madman (Mark Twain had once called him "insane") with delusions of grandeur, a caricature his Wall Street enemies had circulated throughout his presidency to undercut his popularity. In fact, from Hollywood's treatment of Roosevelt (often as a comic figure, as in Robin Williams's 2006 portrayal in *Night at the Museum*), one would hardly guess he was a dignified, sober-minded statesman who commanded the respect of the world. Germany and Japan certainly took him seriously when he threatened them with the might of the U.S. Navy in 1902 and 1907, respectively (in the Venezuelan Crisis and a Japanese war scare), and forced both to back down. So did Britain when TR moved U.S. troops to the Alaskan border during tense negotiations to resolve a boundary dispute between the United States and Canada, gaining everything he demanded.

In the 1950s, when Roosevelt's presidential papers were fully opened and an eight-volume set of his letters was published, historians began to realize how distorted his reputation had become since his death thirty years before. As a result, a much-needed scholarly reassessment of his presidency cast aside the clownish image, emphasizing for the first time the conservative core of his leadership and revealing a serious leader with a brilliant mind. Walter Lippmann, the renowned political commentator and a founder of the liberal *New Republic*, described the real TR when he pointed out a simple truth, that "Theodore Roosevelt was a conservative who adopted progressive policies."[11]

Changing global conditions helped burnish this positive, accurate view of TR. As America assumed the leadership of the free world in the Cold War struggle against Soviet communism, Roosevelt's faith in his country's destiny as a great power seemed far-sighted rather than far-fetched. Despite the international tensions of the 1950s, the American people were optimistic and prosperous and well-disposed to an oracle of national greatness.

The presidency of John F. Kennedy revived the spirit of Theodore Roosevelt. The Massachusetts aristocrat, a war hero and prize-winning author with hawkish views on foreign policy and progressive rhetoric on civil rights and conservation, recalled the Harvard man who had served in the White House sixty years before and had governed the nation as a stealth conservative. Pointing out the remarkable similarities between the two men, one astute observer wrote at the beginning of JFK's administration, "Here is a tale of a wealthy young President, virile, patriotic, widely read, liberal in speech and writing, but conservative on basic issues and never far in front of the public. Does it sound familiar? Perhaps a canny buyer will get a hint of just which past President a history-conscious John F. Kennedy may have chosen for a model."[12]

When the optimistic mood of the country deteriorated after the assassination of Kennedy and the escalation of the Vietnam War, the reputation of the bellicose Roosevelt fell back to earth. By the end of the tumultuous 1960s, conservatives eager to return the country to Harding-esque "normalcy" viewed him with suspicion, seeing his activism as the inspiration for the excesses of Lyndon Johnson's Great Society. At the same time, liberals became disenchanted, especially with the unenlightened racial attitudes that Roosevelt shared with his generation. Not surprisingly, the anti-war movement recoiled from his glorification of war as a beneficial, character-building endeavor. The tide of disfavor against Roosevelt peaked in the late 1970s, when protests erupted in Panama against the American presence on the isthmus, reminding a new generation of the crowbar methods by which he had obtained control of the Panama Canal Zone from Colombia in 1903.

A REAGAN-ERA REVIVAL

Roosevelt's reputation began to rise again with the appearance of two books about his early life. Both Edmund Morris's *The Rise of*

Theodore Roosevelt (1979), winner of the Pulitzer Prize, and David McCullough's *Mornings on Horseback* (1981), winner of the National Book Award, brilliantly captured the swashbuckling appeal that had made Theodore Roosevelt so popular with the American people.

About the same time, Ronald Reagan stepped into the Oval Office and began to pursue policies that reminded many Americans of TR's Big Stick diplomacy. Roosevelt, who had doubled the size of the navy and sent his Great White Fleet on a voyage around the world, surely would have approved of Reagan's plans for a six-hundred-ship navy, dramatically increased military spending, and eagerness to challenge the Soviet Union. These policies fit perfectly with TR's philosophy of deterrence (which Reagan expressed succinctly as "peace through strength"), and they were promoted in the same unequivocal moral terms—the American "shining city on a hill" versus the Soviet "evil empire"—that Roosevelt habitually used when describing enemies, foreign and domestic.

Equally important, the revival of the American economy during the 1980s created a positive national mood that bolstered Roosevelt's standing just as it had in the prosperous 1950s. The country's resurgent optimism made it receptive to the idea of American exceptionalism, the belief in national greatness Roosevelt had trumpeted to the world when he called the United States "the mightiest Republic upon which the sun has ever shone."[13]

The renewed enthusiasm for Roosevelt continued through the 1990s, reaching an apex in 2001 when President Bill Clinton posthumously conferred on him the Medal of Honor for his bravery in the Spanish-American War. Roosevelt had not been shy about his desire for the award, which he considered "the greatest distinction open to any American."[14] He lobbied hard for it after the war, telling his friend Henry Cabot Lodge, "This will seem very egotistical. I am entitled to the Medal of Honor, and I want it."[15] But having made enemies in the War Department, he would not enjoy during his lifetime the country's highest recognition of valor—recognition that any impartial judge would conclude was his due.

Two frustrating and inconclusive wars in the Middle East and a lackluster economy since the financial crisis of 2008 have brought another downturn in the national mood, and Roosevelt's optimism once again seems out of place. To those dismayed by the dramatic growth of the leviathan state, TR's confidence in the power of government to strengthen the country and improve the condition of the American people may seem dated, and even foolish. To those weary of the immense (and apparently futile) sacrifice of blood and treasure in Iraq and Afghanistan, his insistence that the United States should not shirk the responsibilities of a great power may sound like mindless hubris. Conservatives, shortsightedly, seem inclined to abandon Roosevelt, while liberals, perhaps surprisingly—but sensing his continued latent appeal as one of the four presidents on Mount Rushmore—have tried to claim him as one of their own, grabbing onto his achievements as a reformer and conservationist in order to advance their own agenda. Lost in these various caricatures is the true man, a man with giant virtues and perhaps equally great failings, but an unmistakable giant in American history.

CHAPTER TWO

DELIGHTED DEFENDER OF FAMILY AND COUNTRY

~

I f one speech captures the character of the first modern president, it is Roosevelt's address to his supporters just before the Republican National Convention in 1912.

About to be robbed of his party's nomination and infuriated at the certainty of defeat, he electrified a packed Chicago Auditorium (another multitude of supporters was gathered outside): "Assuredly the fight will go on whether we win or lose.... The victory shall be ours, and it shall be won as we have already won so many victories, by clean and honest fighting for the loftiest of causes. We fight in honorable fashion for the good of mankind, fearless for the future, unheeding of our individual fates, with unflinching hearts and undimmed eyes. We stand at Armageddon and we battle for the Lord."[1]

Today such rhetoric comes across as stunningly moralistic, the sort of thing one would expect from a religious extremist. That was not Roosevelt's intent or belief, but it exemplifies why one scholar, Joshua David Hawley, has called him a "preacher of righteousness." Roosevelt's own view of himself was not as a preacher, but as a soldier-statesman who brought his martial spirit to his high-minded ideals.

Roosevelt embraced combat in the political arena with relish, winning victories over the capitalist titans of the age, J. P. Morgan and John D. Rockefeller, as well as an army of lesser combatants including populist Democrats (William Jennings Bryan), corrupt machine bosses (Thomas Platt), stalwart spoils-men (John Wanamaker), demagogic newspaper moguls (William Randolph Hearst), vitriolic pundits (Frank Hatton), rivals on the right (Mark Hanna), rivals on the left (Robert LaFollette), doctrinaire socialists (Eugene Debs), cutthroat bureaucrats (Russell Alger), unctuous hangers-on (Mr. & Mrs. Bellamy Storer), reactionary U.S. senators (Nelson Aldrich), anarchist-friendly governors (John Altgeld), disloyal protégés (William Howard Taft), and insubordinate generals (Nelson Miles). Summing up the combative pattern of TR's political career, one newspaper writer observed, "Where Mr. Roosevelt goes, there quarrelling and wrangling follows."[2]

TR's rapier wit helped him prevail in these contests. By the time he reached the White House, he had probably read more books than any other American president; that study paid off handsomely. A master of the English language, he commanded a vast vocabulary. As someone who knew him said, in his hands "a dead phrase became a political missile. There it lay. There it had always lain. Roosevelt stumbled on it, looked at it, roared, picked it up, hurled it at the right mark, and exploded it into fame."[3] Thus Woodrow Wilson became a "Byzantine logothete"[4] (translation: a passive bureaucrat) because he refused to lead the United States into World War I against Germany during the first years of that contest.

In Roosevelt's hands, witty invective was an assassin's dagger. As jagged as his public comments could be, his private remarks were often savage. The novelist Henry James was "an emasculated mass of inanity"[5]; the German-born reformer Carl Schurz a "prattling foreign reptile"[6]; Postmaster General John Wanamaker "an ill-constitutioned creature, oily, but with bristles sticking up through the oil"[7]; Civil Service Commissioner Charles Lyman "the most intolerably slow and pompous old muttonhead who ever adored red tape"[8]; a justice of New York's highest court "an amiable old fuzzy-wuzzy with sweetbread brains"[9]; Secretary of State William Jennings Bryan "a professional yodeler, a human trombone"[10]; Senator William Peffer "a well-meaning, pinheaded, anarchist crank of hirsute and slabsided aspect"[11]; Secretary of the Interior Hoke Smith, "boisterous, vulgar … who has some power and more shiftiness with his villainous little pigs eyes"[12]; William Randolph Hearst's *New York Journal* a "leprous spot upon our civilization"[13]; Mississippi Congressman John Sharp Williams "the true old-style Jeffersonian of the barbaric blatherskite variety"[14]; Vice President Thomas Hendricks "one of the arch-snakes from the old Copperhead nest."[15]

THE LOVABLE TEDDY BEAR

In anyone else, such an acerbic tongue might have proved repellant, but TR could charm as easily as he could offend, and his offensiveness was almost part of his rambunctious, boyish appeal. Both friends and enemies were drawn to his irresistible force. As one friend said: "To be with him was not simply to live more strivingly. It was to live more abundantly. A primrose by the river's brim became a prodigious episode in the migration of flowers. A shy child coming into the room became a romp and a riot. A feather on the White House lawn a sure sign of the migration of fox-sparrows."[16]

Unlike George Washington, who was awkward to be around because of his monarchial reserve, Roosevelt was friendly and engaging, more like the card-playing Henry Clay than the Puritan-iceberg John Quincy Adams. He was as intellectually curious as Thomas Jefferson, as impatient and aggressive as Andrew Jackson, and had his own inimitable love of nature and family. His sophomoric humor, however, was not always appreciated. Among his favorite pranks: dropping behind those who didn't keep up while horseback riding, and then sprinting forward at a hard gallop, "shouting a cowboy 'Whoopee!'" as he passed. Henry Cabot Lodge, the poster-child for humorless WASPs, was a frequent victim of this rearguard assault, hanging "grimly onto the pommel"[17] of his saddle as the president laughed in sadistic satisfaction that he had melted the gelid dignity of his patrician friend.

Explaining Roosevelt's antics, his British friend Cecil Spring-Rice said: "You must always remember that the President is about six."[18] It was an opinion shared by TR's sardonic secretary of war, Elihu Root, who needled TR on the president's forty-sixth birthday: "You have made a good start in life and your friends have great hopes for you when you grow up."[19] Six years later in 1910, Root had not changed his mind: "Theodore, you are still the same great, overgrown boy as ever."[20] The press appreciated his youthful spirit, too. "He faced every phase of his Presidential life with the bubbling enthusiasm of a schoolboy," wrote the *London Times*.[21] Even Roosevelt's archenemy, Woodrow Wilson, admitted the exuberance of his political foe was endearing. "He is a great big boy," Wilson remarked after a meeting at the White House in 1917. "I was charmed by his personality. There was a sweetness about him that is very compelling. You can't resist the man."[22]

When wielding power, TR enjoyed devilish fun at the expense of wrongdoers. After an army colonel made public remarks that displeased him, "the officer received sudden orders to report to Camp Grant, Arizona. Accompanied only by a Negro orderly, he arrived at this new post to find an all but totally abandoned garrison, consisting of only a few Indian scouts."[23] He was equally creative as police commissioner of New York City when a notorious anti-Semite rabble-rouser demanded police protection. "I decided that the best thing to do was to have him protected by forty Jewish policemen," Roosevelt said later. "Of course it was my duty to see that he was not molested, and it struck me to have him protected by the very members of the race he was denouncing was the most effective answer to that denunciation."[24]

To encounter Roosevelt was to meet a moving object—a whirling dervish in a frock coat who lit up every gloomy bureaucratic workplace with an electric luminescence. One witness waiting for him described how TR "shot through the outer office like a dull brown streak, incidentally firing a question at the pretty secretary as he passed" and that when they finally met, his handshake was "quick, nervous and full of an energy which almost seemed to overflow at touch"[25] and that his greeting was "emphatic, decisive, the syllables chopped off, clean and sharp, as if by a knife."[26] As governor of New York, his ceaseless motion was noted by another witness: "As he works, he must range, now here, now there, ever on his feet, save for brief moments.... Gesticulating, every muscle on tension, at this second frowning, at that laughing, filling the entire room with his presence, he steps back and forth the live-long day."[27]

Roosevelt was as Thomas Carlyle said of Daniel Webster, "a steam engine in trousers,"[28] but at the same time so needful of others he would halt his locomotive ambitions whenever he could to engage in conversation—of course, he always did most of the talking. Senators accustomed to whispering deals in smoke-filled rooms complained about his openness. "The President talks too loudly, giving no chance of privacy,"[29] they whined, pining for the discreet suavity of his predecessor, McKinley. "He is a man who speaks with Bismarckian frankness," wrote the correspondent of the *London Times*, who was struck by Roosevelt's "quick, impatient, yet tolerant look in the eyes, which before you speak seems to say, 'I know what you are going to say and will tell you where you are wrong.'"[30] "The President employs no useless frills in learning what his callers want,"[31] another eyewitness observed, noting the brusque manner in which he conducted business and how he dispensed with daily tasks as though he were mowing down an enemy with a machine gun.

A NIAGARA FALLS OF WORDS, WORDS, WORDS

Possessing a prodigious appetite for both food and talk, Roosevelt would share almost anything on his mind. Surprised the habit hadn't hurt his career, he told historian William Dodd over a noon meal: "When I think of all the things I have said, all the mistakes even, I am surprised that I am President." He was alluding to the fact that outspoken leaders rarely rise to the highest office in the land. In the historian's opinion, Roosevelt was "blunt, quick and outspoken," but Dodd thought these qualities had actually helped his lunch companion, telling TR, "it is just because of what you have said, Mr. President, and what you have done that you are President."[32]

Dodd glossed over the numerous verbal landmines Roosevelt had inadvertently stepped on over the years. For instance, Roosevelt once called Thomas Paine a "filthy little atheist,"[33] a remark he was forced to explain all his life. While defending Christendom against the slurs of the infidel Paine, he also warred against pacifists whose consciences would not permit combat engagement, declaring: "In the long run, a Quaker may be quite as undesirable a citizen as is a duelist. No man who is not willing to bear arms and to fight for his rights can give a good reason why he should be entitled to the privilege of living in a free community."[34] Attacking agitators who said too much (Paine) and pacifists who did too little (Quakers), Roosevelt's assaults on those he disagreed with revealed his habit of firing howitzer-like denunciations at either side of the political spectrum, depending on which was gaining strength at a given moment. At his core, he was a conservative who frowned on all threats to the social order, whether they came from the left or the right. Above all else, he valued a healthy balance of power, not only to avoid war between nations, but also in the domestic sphere so that the country could thrive without social unrest endangering peace and prosperity.

While Roosevelt's gaffes are forgotten, his love of *delighted* is not. He repeated the word at least fifty times a day, pronouncing it as if it were three separate words, as do his impersonators. "He is 'dee-light-ed' to see you," noted one eyewitness of the president's verbal tick, "'dee-light-ed' to hear you are well and 'dee-light-ed' everything else." He also overused superlatives (fitting for one with a superlative personality), especially "very," which he sprinkled liberally throughout speeches. For emphasis in conversation, he would blurt out "By Jove!" and "By George!" whenever he got excited, which was often.[35]

The peculiar words that flowed from Roosevelt's mouth were matched by equally peculiar commentary gushing from his pen. Seeing himself as an oracle of wisdom who knew better than anyone the best course for the country, he loved dispensing advice, deluging the nation in "a Niagara of words, words, words" that was breathtaking.[36] His turgid annual messages to Congress, cumulatively about as long as a Russian novel, contained pearls that set him apart from his less-verbose predecessors, who invariably confined their remarks on the State of the Union to regurgitations of tariff-revenue figures and facts equally lifeless. A windbag Polonius, the young president could not restrain his pen when his turn came to lecture Congress, informing the legislature, among other things, that it would be best to create preserves "for the wild forest creatures"; that women who used birth control committed "a sin for which there is no atonement"; that militarism was a "non-existent evil" which had "not the slightest chance of appearing here"; that wife beaters should themselves be beaten as punishment; that the multimillionaire "whose son is a fool and his daughter a princess" was the moral equivalent of a "marauder baron of the dark ages"; that immigrants with "a low moral tendency or of unsavory reputation" should not be allowed into the country.[37]

President Roosevelt was a fiery pepper in the sometimes bland stew of politics. Not everyone welcomed his burning advice. It reminded them of years before his presidency when he disturbed the tranquility of Washington, on one occasion telling a reporter that radical leftists should be put up against a wall and shot. "We know him of old as a person in whom the craving for notoriety is very slightly, if at all, tempered by prudence and self-restraint," wrote the *Washington Post*, referring to his advocacy for firing-squad justice. "He has taken many prizes ...as the very Prince of Bumptiousness and the High Priest of Brutal Arrogance. Habitually, he is a well-mannered, well-educated, quick-witted gentleman. Sporadically, he is perhaps the most thoroughly Boeotian hoodlum who has ever been smuggled into polite society."[38]

ALWAYS TIME FOR ORDINARY FOLK AND HIS CHILDREN

With his Jupiter-sized ego, genius-level IQ, and genteel pedigree, he might have stood aloof and sneered at the hoi polloi, but he did not.

While traveling aboard a battleship to visit Panama in 1906, he astonished the vessel's officers by "going down in one of the fire rooms to shovel coal,"[39] brute labor not expected of the president. But he executed the drudgery with relish, sweating side-by-side with the lowest members of the crew in the ship's dungeon-like belly. Episodes like these, which abound throughout his career, revealed his Lincolnesque ability to connect with regular folks. He revealed he was one of them, that he understood their challenges, and empathized with their condition.

The Japanese diplomat Kentaro Kaneko captured Roosevelt's human touch with this anecdote about his visit to Sagamore Hill describing the president's hospitality after a long dinner conversation:

> The President rose and lit the candle, and conducted me upstairs to my room. It was a cool night. He felt the coverings on my bed and decided that I might need another blanket. "I'll get you one," he said, leaving the room. And in a minute or two he reappeared with a blanket over his shoulder. "Come," he said, as he put it on the bed, "and I'll show you the bath room." I went with him. "Here's soap," said he, "and here are clean towels." Then he took me back to my room and wished me a good night.

Kaneko was stunned; the president had assumed tasks other heads of state would leave to servants. He declared that the display of simple manners had given him "as great an honor as a man could have."[40]

Roosevelt could snap a crisp "Make it so!"[41] using the nautical language of a navy commander when informed the Great White Fleet was ready to begin its voyage, and then in the next breath tell a diplomat from the nation most threatened by the sixteen battleships: "Here's soap and here are clean towels." TR could be both authoritative and humble in the same breath. One great source of strength that allowed him to do that was his family. He was the unmistakable head of his household, who also adored his wife and doted on his children. William Howard Taft observed: "We never had a President whose family life has been better than Roosevelt's. The people know it. That's why they like him."[42]

TR was a remarkable father, always finding time to play with his six children as he went about conquering the universe, leading them on boisterous hikes in Rock Creek Park in Washington or the Oyster Bay woods around Sagamore Hill. He could also be a martinet, riding his oldest so hard as a boy that Ted Jr. had a nervous breakdown. "If one of my boys was a bully, I'd try to thrash it out of him," said Roosevelt. "If he would not defend himself against a bully, I'd thrash him until I had some degree of manhood in him. He'd require but one thrashing."[43] As harsh as his approach to parenting might sound, he demonstrated immense love of his children; they worshipped him in return as a figure of absolute authority who was also fun to be around.

None of TR's sons became a renowned statesmen, but all demonstrated a behavior he highly valued: battlefield heroics. He and his oldest son Ted Jr. are, along with Arthur and Douglas MacArthur, the only father-and-son pairs to win the Congressional Medal of Honor; his second son, Kermit, served with distinction in the Middle East during World War I; his third son, Archie, recovered from crippling wounds received in both world wars after demonstrating valor during each conflict; his youngest son, Quentin, died in battle when his plane was shot down in France in 1918. Given these military records, no other president can be mentioned in the same breath with TR as a father of heroes. He never felt proud of his merchant ancestors who stood on the sidelines during the Revolutionary War, the War of 1812, the Mexican War, and the Civil War. But the courage and sacrifice of his sons (three of them died in uniform) more than redeemed his ancestors' failure to risk life-and-limb for their country during its formative years.

MAKING THE MOST OF ALL GOD GAVE HIM

TR's courage, which all his sons inherited, was a trait he developed battling childhood asthma. In that struggle, he worked hard to put muscle on a frail physique; and he refused to indulge in self-pity.

As a young man, Roosevelt was devastated when his mother died of typhoid fever and his wife of undiagnosed Bright's disease within eleven hours of each other in the same house. He escaped into the West, becoming a cattle rancher in the Dakota Territory. "Black care rarely sits behind a rider whose pace is fast enough,"[44] he said as he rode the roundup and stalked grizzly bears, using the tasks as an anodyne to soothe his wounded soul and bury a terrible loss under a whirlwind of strenuous activity.

Stoic and resilient, he never let setbacks derail his ambitions; and one source of his resilience was his love of nature, which to him was a restorative. He loved, for example, anything to do with birds, especially their songs. To him, a meadowlark was Beethoven and a nightingale Mozart, providing, along with their aviary brethren, the classical music of the natural world. During early morning horseback rides in Oyster Bay, a symphony of chirps from "robins, wood thrushes, catbirds, song sparrows, chipping sparrows, grasshopper finches and Baltimore orioles"[45] would bolster his spirit for the busy day ahead. In Washington, he would "stand motionless under trees" on the White House lawn for long periods, puzzling the groundskeepers who were unaware the president was a published ornithologist.[46]

Squarely and heavily built, Roosevelt, with the body of a sturdy dwarf from Tolkien's *Lord of the Rings* and a "jaw suggestive of a bulldog," was anything but a bird-loving poet in appearance.[47] Hardened by years of physical activity that had developed his barrel chest well into middle age, his physique softened during his presidency as he gained weight around the middle, giving him a portly appearance when leaving the White House in 1909. That he put on pounds was not surprising, given his prodigious appetite. His chief of forestry, Gifford Pinchot, marveled that the president "ate nearly twice as much as the average man."[48]

Physically, Roosevelt may not have won the genetic lottery, but he was born with a compensating gift, an extraordinary brain: analytical in the keen insights it regularly churned out and capacious in the vast amount of knowledge it stored. His soaring intellect placed him in the elite company of other scholarly presidents, including Jefferson, Madison, John and John Quincy Adams, Garfield, and Wilson. According to

Supreme Court Justice Felix Frankfurter, who personally knew every president from McKinley to Kennedy, Roosevelt was "the nearest to an egghead" among them.[49] His mind had only one hole: an ignorance of finance and economics the size of the Grand Canyon. In this respect, he was the inverse of Alexander Hamilton, who would have cringed at Roosevelt's admission, "when it comes to finance or compound differentials, I am all up in the air."[50]

Roosevelt did not think in terms of numbers but rather animals. An accomplished faunal naturalist who shot, killed, stuffed, and mounted any bird that flew by him in childhood—and a trophy-seeking hunter who killed bears, antelope, and elk for sport into manhood—he habitually mixed the political world with the animal kingdom. Thus, when Britain sent Mortimer Durand, a haughty diplomat with limited mental capacity to Washington, the president complained: "Why under Heaven the English keep him here I do not know! ...He seems to have a brain of about eight-guinea-pig-power!"[51] When President Castro of Venezuela (the Hugo Chavez of that generation) made trouble in the Caribbean, he became "an unspeakable villainous little monkey."[52] And when the pacifist playwright Bernard Shaw hampered the war effort against Germany during World War I, he was denounced as a timid "blue-rumped ape."[53]

LOVE OF FAMILY, LOVE OF COUNTRY

As much as Roosevelt was driven by wide-ranging intellectual curiosity, he did not have a wandering eye. His diary documents his relentless pursuit of his first wife, the head-turning socialite, Alice Hathaway Lee, and the rapid courtship of her enigmatic, plain-Jane successor, Edith Carow. But after that, no lurid tales exist of his trying to seduce other men's wives as Thomas Jefferson did more than once. Instead, we see another George Washington, who was faithful to Martha, and John Adams, who was faithful to Abigail. Neither lothario nor satyr, he was nonetheless a passionate and romantic man, who imprinted moving poetry like Robert Browning's "Love Among the Ruins" onto his soul.

"I so firmly believe that all other success, once the means of actual subsistence have been secured, counts for nothing compared to the success of the man in winning the one woman who is all the world to him,"[54] he declared, adding that "love is best"—the last line of Browning's poem—summed up the whole matter.

Roosevelt loved his country as a faithful man loves his wife, defining his patriotism as "the pride of personal possession"[55] and viewing treason as a crime similar to marital infidelity (treason was worse; it affected the nation and not merely a family). "Love of country is an elemental virtue, like love of home, or like honesty or courage,"[56] he declared. Rejecting cosmopolitanism as the moral equivalent of polygamy, he said, "the man who loves other countries as much as he does his own is quite as noxious a member of society as the man who loves other women as much as he loves his wife."[57] For this reason, TR could never tolerate Americans like the novelist Henry James who renounced their citizenship to become British nationals or the daughters of American millionaires who married British lords to gain a royal title (he disliked Winston Churchill in part because the British statesman's mother, the Brooklyn-born Jenny Jerome, had followed this path).

Roosevelt's character was chivalrous, combining a romantic belief that "love is best," with a desire to protect the weak and vulnerable, and an admonition to West Point cadets that "a good soldier must not only be willing to fight, but must be anxious to fight."[58] TR's sense of chivalry extended to animals. Once, when he was "marching to church," he "suddenly saw two terriers racing to attack a kitten which was walking down the sidewalk." "I bounced forward with my umbrella, and after some active work put to flight the dogs." He gave the kitten, "a friendly, helpless little thing," to a little girl who "welcomed it lovingly."[59]

Roosevelt also intervened to save struggling poets, notably the future literary great Edwin Arlington Robinson, whose poetry had been recommended to TR by his son Kermit (a student at the time at Groton). Upon learning the poet was barely making a living in a Boston millinery store writing metrical advertisements for spring hats, TR contacted him. Without being asked, he then promptly gave Robinson a sinecure in the

Treasury Department, stipulating he should concentrate on poetry rather than government work. TR bypassed civil-service laws he had long championed requiring that government jobs be awarded via competitive examination. But, as he said on another occasion, "A poet may do far more for a country than the owner of a nail factory,"[60] or, perhaps he would have added, than a clerk in the civil service.

Many political figures stand apart from the nation, but not Roosevelt. As his British friend Lord Morley told Lady Harcourt: "He is not an American, you know, he *is America*."[61] One-part Jeffersonian democrat (though he loathed Jefferson), one-part Gallic monarch (though he disdained monarchy), Roosevelt considered himself the perfect patriot whose self-interest was indistinguishable from the national interest, believing he would always use his fame and power not for selfish ends but to increase the strength of the United States. He made mistakes, and as much as he welcomed criticism, he always believed his intentions were pure.

Seeing no difference between the United States and himself, Roosevelt wished everything for his country he wanted for himself: fame, power, and glory. He was far from perfect, but the American people always gave him the benefit of the doubt and overlooked his flaws; they saw that his heart was in the right place. They were right to do so.

CHAPTER THREE

MISCONCEPTIONS ABOUT TR

~

"TR'S IDEOLOGY WAS LIBERALISM"

Conventional wisdom about Theodore Roosevelt revolves around the word *progressive*, synonymous in the modern mind with *liberal*, a word that immediately links him with Democrat icons like Lyndon Johnson, Ted Kennedy, and Barack Obama. But he was not like these statist liberals at all. If you wanted to find the closest match among Democrats of the last hundred years, it would be with John F. Kennedy; among Republicans, Ronald Reagan. All three were masters of the bully pulpit; all three believed in American exceptionalism; all three were conservatives willing to be guided by changing circumstances, making them realists rather than ideologues.

America's founding was based on two competing political philosophies. On the one hand was the eighteenth-century liberalism epitomized by Thomas Jefferson, which saw man as an enlightened being who could rise to new heights if only he were freed from the shackles of religious, political, and intellectual tyranny. On the other hand, Alexander Hamilton took a more conservative view, seeing man as a fallen creature, driven by fear and self-interest. Jefferson sought to empower individual citizens to pursue happiness; Hamilton was more concerned about empowering the state to prevent anarchy.

Roosevelt was a Hamiltonian—a conservative in the eighteenth-century sense of the word. Rather than urging the American people to "pursue happiness," as Jefferson the liberal did in the Declaration of Independence, Roosevelt admonished them to live the "Strenuous Life" of duty, toil, and strife, and to avoid "ignoble ease"—advice Hamilton would have heartily approved.

A "compassionate conservative" a century before the term became a slogan, Roosevelt was deeply concerned about labor strife, impoverished immigrants, racial segregation in the South, and the hardships of those he (and Abraham Lincoln) called "plain people." He had read *How the Other Half Lives* and seen with his own eyes the squalor of the Lower East Side of Manhattan in the early 1890s with the book's author, Jacob Riis, as his guide. Experiences like these, which revealed that the life of many Americans was "nasty, brutish, and short," reinforced TR's conservatism, confirming the Hobbesian realism that formed the foundation of his value system.

But he also believed in progress. He believed that parents who worked hard and sacrificed could improve the lot of their children and grandchildren. He believed that the spirit of *noblesse oblige*, and occasionally government action, could mitigate some of the greater hardships of the poor and the struggling working man. And like many educated people of his day, he bought into tenets of Social Darwinism, leading him to believe that history was the story of civilization's advance. Social Darwinism also influenced Roosevelt's fear of decline. America, which had proven its strength in conquering a continent, had to find ways to maintain that strength and animal vitality. Whereas Jefferson wanted to recreate the enlightened society of Athens, Roosevelt wanted the United States to embrace the grim toughness of ancient Sparta, the apex of a warrior culture.

Roosevelt believed the exemplar of American liberalism, Jefferson, lacked barbarian strength. To him, the peace-loving Sage of Monticello was a contemptible theoretician, an intellectual (like Woodrow Wilson) who lived in his own mind rather than the real world. He was especially critical of Jefferson's decision prior to the War of 1812 to build flimsy, horse-drawn gunboats to protect America's coast instead of building large frigates that could stand toe-to-toe with the British and French navies. "The man who does not face facts is a fool,"[1] said Roosevelt, succinctly stating his opinion of Jefferson and all like him who did not prepare the country for inevitable wars.

Roosevelt had no patience with visionary doctrinaires who tried to impose theoretical schemes on society—"educated ineffectives" as he derisively called them.[2] They pontificated from the ivory towers of academe and socialized in comfortable parlors to advocate remedies, which to him had, like Jefferson's infamous gunboats, "the prime defect of being unworkable."[3] Tellingly, *doctrinaire* was among TR's favorite words (another was *menace*), which he deployed as a stinging pejorative to condemn the intellectual descendants of Jefferson. Roosevelt had the natural conservative preference for experience over ideology. "It is well to keep in mind the remark of Frederick the Great that if he wished to punish a province he would allow it to be governed by philosophers,"[4] he liked to say to emphasize his own practical worldview.

To Theodore Roosevelt, Barack Obama would have been another naïve "parlor intellectual," cut from the same mold as Thomas Jefferson. He would have recoiled at Obama's repudiation of American exceptionalism and shaken his head in disgust at Obama's remarkable statement: "*Whether we like it or not*, we remain a dominant military superpower" [emphasis added]. Roosevelt had no doubts about America's virtue, about the need for American strength, or about the practical gifts America had to offer the world as an imperial power.

Roosevelt the realist did not see democracy as a universal right or panacea. He believed the American people had earned the right to govern themselves as their natural inheritance from the Magna Carta. Other countries did not have the same political grounding or experience. Though opposed to slavery, he once remarked that its perpetuation in Haiti for "a century or so longer" might have been preferable to the sorry effects of "democracy" on that island.[5] The limits of TR's belief in popular government, and also his belief that circumstances can change, can be seen in his rejection of the Democratic Party's proposal that U.S. senators be directly elected by the American people rather than by state legislatures, the process laid down in the Constitution. In 1912, however, he changed his mind and supported the idea in his presidential run on the Progressive platform, because, unlike Alexander Hamilton, he was a populist conservative, whose policies closely tracked the voters' will. In his sensitivity to public opinion at least, TR was unmistakably Jeffersonian.

All of this underlines that while Roosevelt had core principles—including a belief in domestic reform to maintain social stability and in a strong national defense—he was pragmatic in his application of his principles. Such pragmatism meant that different images come to mind when we think of Roosevelt at different points in his political career. At the outset, in the New York Assembly, he was a high-minded corruption fighter and reformer, opposed to political machines, even that of his own party. By the middle of the 1880s, however, he moved right across the political spectrum, becoming a Republican Party loyalist, supporting its candidates, backing its protectionist trade policies against his previous free trade positions, and accepting the support of the party machine in his campaign to become mayor of New York.

By the 1890s, he was back in his role as a crusading reformer as U.S. Civil Service commissioner and even worked for two years in the administration of a Democrat president, albeit a conservative one, Grover Cleveland. Midway through the 1890s, he moved back to the right, as seen in his war against Tammany Hall Democrats, in his law-and-order service as New York City's police commissioner, and in his vitriolic campaign against the Democrat William Jennings Bryan whom he regarded as a dangerous, leftist radical. In foreign policy he was among the most aggressive voices, as assistant secretary of the navy, for declaring war against Spain.

At the turn of the century, he moved back to the left, becoming a reformist governor in New York and then a "trust buster" president, breaking up monopolistic corporations and regulating the railroads. But while a cautious reformer himself, he disdained leftist investigative journalists as "muckrakers," and ordained as his presidential successor the conservative William Howard Taft.

Perhaps the most problematic period for Roosevelt, in terms of his conservatism, was when he became disenchanted with Taft, bolted from the Republican Party, and ran as the candidate of the newly formed Progressive Bull Moose Party. But no sooner had he been defeated as "the progressive" Republican candidate against the Democrat Woodrow Wilson (finishing second, with the GOP nominee, William Howard Taft, finishing third), than he swerved unmistakably right as one of the most fervent critics of the Wilson administration. He rejoined the Republican Party in 1916 and supported its candidate for president, the conservative Charles Evans Hughes, and was at this point in his career so conservative, while still dallying with progressive reforms, that had he lived he could easily have become a unifying Republican Party presidential candidate in 1920.

"TR FAVORED BIG GOVERNMENT"

Present-day libertarian critics of Roosevelt often identify him as the root cause of the country's financial problems. They claim his desire to expand the power of government to promote "social justice" launched a movement that now threatens to push the United States into bankruptcy. But this critique misrepresents Roosevelt's record. It is true that he expanded government, but he did it prudentially, not from an ideological belief that government bureaucracies should intrude into every nook and cranny of American life. His administration was, by today's standards, a model of limited government and frugality.

During his presidency, the country enjoyed a healthy balance sheet, notable for budget surpluses and a modest national debt that was easily serviced, given the nation's rapidly growing economy. For instance, in fiscal year 1903, the federal government took in $694,621,117 in revenue while spending $640,323,450 (92 percent of total revenue), thereby producing a surplus of $54,297,687 (8 percent of total revenue).[6]

These budgetary numbers (typical for his presidency) demonstrate that Theodore Roosevelt governed as a fiscal conservative. His fiscal restraint is especially noticeable when measured by the nation's spending-to-GDP ratio. Today, the federal government spends roughly 20 percent of GDP compared to only 3 percent in 1903—a level nearly seven times higher.

One of Roosevelt's forgotten domestic-policy achievements, the creation of the Reclamation Service to irrigate arid Western regions, embodied his thrifty administration. This massive infrastructure initiative, which opened up sparsely populated areas of the country to new migrants by giving them access to water, was not a Big Government spending scheme in the fashion of the Great Society, but a loan program financed by the sale of public lands, which increased in value once water became available. Although the Reclamation Service was managed by engineers in Washington, it empowered individual states to choose the dams, aqueducts, and other water-related public works they wanted. Each state, in turn, had to pay back the money it borrowed from the U.S. Treasury.

None other than Senator Barry Goldwater of Arizona, the father of the modern conservative movement, later lauded Roosevelt's Reclamation Service for its enduring success.[7] Given libertarian propaganda against Theodore Roosevelt, it might seem that he and Goldwater were strange bedfellows, yet they shared much in common. Roosevelt's focus was primarily on reforming government, not increasing its scope (he could have demanded that Washington dominate the nation's reclamation efforts, but instead gave immense power to individual states). If anything, Roosevelt's social conservatism might put him to the *right* of Goldwater, who at least later in his political career was something of a social liberal.

Roosevelt was a foe of government corruption (rife in the generation that followed the Civil War) and an ardent enemy of the spoils system (which made government inefficient by filling its ranks with political appointees who were often unqualified). He urged the expansion of the country's tiny navy (in 1898, it kept only four battleships afloat) using money from available budget surpluses to finance the construction of new ships. Other than this defense initiative, TR did not advocate any increase in federal spending; had he done so, he certainly would not have aimed at redistributing wealth to lower-income Americans (a position held at that time only by leftist extremists). An income tax on the rich might have been used to that end, but he opposed the levy until popular support for it reached critical mass after he left the White House. He preferred an inheritance tax, not so much to redistribute wealth but to guard against the social (and socialist) unrest that might result from a decadent, self-centered aristocracy of the "idle rich." He wanted no replay of the French Revolution on American soil.

Roosevelt wanted to increase the *power* of government, but he didn't want to increase its size as measured by the quantity of money collected from the population. He never asked the American people to send more money to Washington so that bureaucrats could spend their hard-earned dollars for them. He wanted to increase the regulatory power of government to protect consumers (such objectives cost little money), establishing the Departments of Commerce and Labor to help achieve this goal. He never dreamed of setting up programs like Social Security or Medicare. The expense would have seemed extraordinary and unjustifiable. He never intended for Americans to become *dependent* on government. That would have been demeaning. His entire political philosophy was founded on the idea that Americans should lead the Strenuous Life of duty, hard work, and self-sacrifice. As he declared in a speech shortly before becoming president:

> The only way to help a man is to aid him in helping himself. All of us stumble many times during a lifetime, and the duty of his neighbor is to help him to his feet so he may help himself. You can help a man successfully, but you can't carry him successfully. If you rob a man of his self-respect, take away his sturdy, self-reliant manhood, no good you can do will make amends.[8]

In the first two decades of Roosevelt's career, he was no bleeding-heart champion of "social justice." He stood firmly with conservatives who sought social stability when violent labor strife was common. After a labor protest in Chicago escalated into the infamous Haymarket bombing of 1886, TR assured those closest to him that his sympathies lay with Big Business, not the discontented laboring masses. As he wrote to his sister, the cowboys he employed on his Badlands cattle ranch worked "longer hours for no greater wages than many of the strikers, but they are American through and through. I believe nothing would give them greater pleasure than a chance with their rifles at one of the mobs. I wish I had them with me, and a fair show at ten times our number of rioters. My men shoot well and fear very little."[9]

At this time, Roosevelt was a conservative who wanted government to stave off potentially revolutionary movements and to protect his financial interests, not right social wrongs. As an aristocrat living off of inherited wealth and as the owner of a small business (his ranch), his instincts were to use force, when necessary, to maintain order. He heartily supported Grover Cleveland when the pro-business president used the U.S. Army to break the Pullman Strike in 1894. A decade later, he distanced himself from the wealthy plutocrats who encouraged Cleveland to act as he did; but he was always a conservative opposed to socialism and social unrest.

Roosevelt's conservatism was certainly glaring in his vocal and consistent criticism of the populist Democrat William Jennings Bryan. During the 1896 presidential campaign, Bryan, the Democrat nominee for president, wanted to devalue the currency (to alleviate the financial distress of the nation's farmers), dismantle the protective tariff (which made consumers pay higher prices), and prosecute the nation's monopolistic corporations (which flaunted the Sherman anti-trust law with impunity). Roosevelt crisscrossed the country campaigning against Bryan, declaring him a radical. Roosevelt's own reformist policies were meant in large part to stifle the appeal of Bryan's radical ideas, and by the time Roosevelt reached the White House a few years later, he adroitly commandeered Bryan's attack on the trusts into a form of conservative populism. During his presidency he created a modest regulatory regime to ensure the trusts could not destroy their competitors by fixing railroad shipping rates (the Elkins and Hepburn acts), and enacted laws to protect consumers from tainted meat, food, and drugs. But these achievements were merely a measured response to vociferous public demands; they were not a socialistic transformation of the country's free-market economy as called for by Bryan.

Roosevelt's reformist conservatism had as its goal a government that was responsive to the will of the American people and not the domain of wealthy special interests who could dictate policy to compliant politicians. In the pattern of Alexander Hamilton, he favored a lean-and-mean government that was highly efficient and financially stable, and strong enough to propel the United States forward to become the world's greatest power.

Roosevelt's reformist agenda was meant to ensure that socialist parties, platforms, and policies did not gain traction in the United States. At his core, he was a conservative patriot who was proud of his country; he was a religious and social conservative who saw faith and family as essential to America's character; and he was a traditionalist conservative who cherished America's ideals. He was the opposite of today's multicultural globalists who consider the Christian West the bane of civilization.

Roosevelt thought religious belief was essential to an orderly society, which of necessity rested on virtue and self-restraint. He urged Americans to live according to the rules of Judeo-Christian morality, to read the Bible regularly, and to faithfully attend church services so that scriptural lessons could be continuously absorbed; he set the example by attending church with his family every Sunday.

He denounced divorce, birth control, and polygamy as assaults on the natural family. He would certainly have opposed invented rights to same-sex marriage, which he would have considered an oxymoron, if not an encouragement to vice. As police commissioner of New York City, he declared war on the illicit sex industry, arresting prostitutes, pimps, and johns.

He favored curbing alcohol abuse by imposing a "high license fee" on sellers, and he virtually disowned his brother Elliott when he became a drunken playboy and fathered an out-of-wedlock child with an Irish servant girl. Theodore Roosevelt was outspoken about the duty of being responsible—not just personally, but for one's family and community.

He was a man of law and order. As governor of New York, he granted far fewer pardons to convicted criminals than his predecessors. As president he spoke out against lynching, and he was renowned for enforcing moribund laws that other leaders ignored, like the Pendleton Act (on civil service reform), the Raines Law (to curb alcohol abuse), and the Sherman Anti-Trust Act. But equally he believed in providing a check on the potentially arbitrary power of judges. In 1912, he proposed that the American people be given the power to recall unpopular judicial decisions of state courts that involved constitutional questions. It is easy to imagine him today railing against "judicial tyranny" as just another form of the "invisible government" of special interests, party bosses, and political machines that he campaigned against in his own day.

TR's libertarian critics denounce him for expanding government, but fail to realize that his real goal was to maximize the power of the American people as the sovereign of the nation. To this end, he favored additional checks on government power, encouraging states to adopt or allow, as a reform measure, ballot initiatives, electoral referenda, and recall campaigns so that the public would not be subject to legislatures and courts that flaunted their authority against the people.

Roosevelt was a prudent guardian of the public purse on several levels—he governed as a fiscal conservative; he condemned governments that repudiated their debts; and he declared his famous Roosevelt Corollary to the Monroe Doctrine to ensure that Latin American nations paid their financial debts to European creditors. He rejected socialistic schemes, like those of William Jennings Bryan, for the government to take over the nation's railroads. TR's policy of regulating Big Business was, in fact, meant as a vigorous defense of private property, pitting modest (conservative) reforms against the proposals of left-wing extremists like Bryan. Roosevelt also issued an executive order that declared unions could not force government workers into their ranks, proving that he was not the puppet of the labor movement. His desire was always to give what he called a "Square Deal" to both labor and capital.

In economics, as in all else, Roosevelt wanted to make America stronger, and he saw monopolistic corporations as impediments to the effective operation of free markets. When it came to his famous conservation policies, it should be remembered that he favored the development of Alaska's mineral wealth; and he wished to harvest the nation's forests as if they were crops and then replant them. His chief concern was not nature worship, though he loved the outdoors and natural beauty, but that the country use its natural resources wisely and not recklessly deplete them—the very definition of a conservative policy.

He regarded foreign trade as a means to increase the economic strength of the United States as well. The "Open Door" to commerce with China was a pillar of his foreign policy. That did not, however, mean an "open door" to unrestricted immigration to the United States. Roosevelt did not regard an influx of cheap labor as a good thing. He thought America's immigration policy should be highly selective. As he said: "We cannot have too many immigrants of the right kind. We should have none at all of the wrong kind."[10] To this end, he extended the Chinese Exclusion Act and negotiated a "gentleman's agreement" with Japan to keep Asian "coolies" out of the country.

Roosevelt's promotion of American strength was most obvious in his foreign policy. He dramatically increased the size of the navy, expanded its range of operation by building the Panama Canal, sent the Great White Fleet around the world to showcase American power, and championed the idea of an American empire extending across the North American continent to the Philippines. From his bully pulpit he praised soldiers who displayed heroism in combat, aiming to increase the "fighting edge" of the nation. To that same end, he unhesitatingly supported Americans' Second Amendment right to gun ownership so that they could hunt and protect themselves. The "gun room" of his Sagamore Hill home contained a small arsenal of firearms. He carried a concealed revolver during and after his presidency, and when shot in the chest by a would-be assassin in 1912, he did not blame the easy availability of guns—indeed he was dismissive of the assassination attempt itself, proceeding to give a campaign speech for an hour with a .38 caliber bullet in his body.

Anyone who calls Theodore Roosevelt a liberal should be reminded that his closest political allies, the three men he trusted most to lead the United States—Elihu Root, William Howard Taft, and Henry Cabot Lodge—were deeply conservative men, each of whom opposed him during the 1912 presidential election when he bolted from the Republican Party to run as a Progressive. Prior to that split, they were the "Four Musketeers" of American politics, bonded together by a fervent nationalism, with Mr. Roosevelt and Mr. Taft "known as D'Artagnan and Porthos to their intimates during Mr. Roosevelt's presidency, Messrs. Root and Lodge being the other two Musketeers, as their Washington friends called them."[11]

Elihu Root, one of the most respected corporate lawyers in the country and hardly an apologist for TR given his later break from him, accurately assessed Roosevelt's presidency when he declared in 1904: "I say that he has been during these years since President McKinley's death the greatest conservative force for the protection of property and our institutions in the city of Washington."[12] TR, for his part, wished his highly conservative colleague could have been president, declaring a few years later: "I would walk on my hands and knees from the White House to the Capitol to see Root made President, but it cannot be done. He couldn't be elected."[13]

That Roosevelt would want one of the country's leading conservatives to succeed him in 1909 suggests that he was more concerned with consolidating the progressive gains he achieved during his presidency than initiating new ones. That he preferred a conservative like Root for the presidency, and then installed another conservative in the White House, Taft, and urged the nomination of yet another conservative, Lodge, as the 1916 Republican presidential candidate says the same. TR was a reformer and friendly with many left-wing activists like Jane Addams, but his closest political allies, his brain-trust, was planted firmly right of center.

"TR WAS AN IMPERIALIST WARMONGER"

Given the misconception that Roosevelt loved war, the nickname that stands out in the 1909 *Baltimore Sun* survey is "the Peacemaker" (fifth on the top-ten list). We picture TR charging up Kettle Hill during the Spanish-American War; we see him mounting his bully pulpit to preach righteous war as a noble endeavor; we regard him as the apostle of an American empire. But his bellicose persona can mislead us. When his presidency ended, the American people thought of him as both a peacemaker *and* a warrior ("the Rough Rider" was the sixth-favorite nickname). To understand this seeming contradiction, we must distinguish between Roosevelt the man and Roosevelt the president. His desire to hurl his own body into battle was always greater than his desire to push the country into war.

Living in the generation that followed the Civil War, he was saturated with tales of valor and sacrifice made by the soldiers who fought in that horrific conflict; he came to see these heroes as the embodiment of the virtuous strength essential to any great nation. His own father and uncles, New York merchants devoted to peaceful commerce, paid $300 each to hire substitutes to avoid risking their lives for the Union cause, which they supported from the sidelines. Those choices set up a striking contrast—the praiseworthy courage of warriors versus the ignoble passivity of merchants—that fueled his lifelong desire to be associated with the soldiers. "No merchant, no banker, no railroad magnate, no inventor of improved industrial processes, can do for any nation what can be done for it by its fighting men,"[14] he declared, in an implied rebuke of his own father and uncles, adding, "it is better for a nation to produce one Grant or one Farragut than a thousand shrewd manufacturers or successful speculators."[15]

He wanted the United States to retain the rugged strength that it had shown during its westward expansion of the frontier in order to keep the country at the top of the world's geopolitical food chain. Like Alexander Hamilton, he never wanted the United States to be at the mercy of, or dependent on, other nations. The other two rising powers in the world,

Japan (with its Samurai warrior code) and Germany (with its "blood-and-iron" Prussian strength) had shown prowess on the battlefield; he was adamant that the United States must foster a similar culture to remain competitive.

"My impression is that Roosevelt's view on the subject of war and peace is a sincere attitude. He loves war," said William Howard Taft, a few months after World War I began. "He thinks it is essential to develop the highest traits of manhood and he believes in forcible rather than peaceable methods. That is his temperament, his nature."[16] Taft was correct: Roosevelt believed individual men benefited from combat experience. But Taft's caricature implies that TR rejected diplomacy as a tool to resolve international conflict. Nothing could be further from the truth. During his presidency, his masterful handling of American foreign policy kept the country out of any new wars (U.S. troops were already fighting insurrectionists in the Philippines when TR entered the White House in 1901).

An examination of Roosevelt's stellar record as a peacemaker obliterates the persistent misconception that he was a warmonger; in fact, his efforts to promote international peace are unmatched by any other president. All told, he prevented at least three wars from starting, limited the scope of another that was under way, and mediated diplomatic negotiations to end a major war between Russia and Japan. He has never received sufficient credit for all of these remarkable accomplishments.

Roosevelt's first notable success as a statesman devoted to peace came in 1902 when war between the United States and Germany threatened over the latter's naval blockade of Venezuela to settle a financial dispute. Rather than publicly denounce Germany for violating the Monroe Doctrine, and thereby gin up a crisis that would have escalated into war, he used quiet diplomacy and the threat of overwhelming American naval power to persuade Kaiser Wilhelm II to settle differences with Venezuela through arbitration.

Then when Germany and France seemed on the verge of entering the Russo-Japanese war on Russia's side, Roosevelt warned both nations that if they took that extraordinary step, he would bring the United States into the conflict on the side of Japan to safeguard the balance of power in Asia and American commercial interests in Manchuria, which were secured by the Open Door to China's lucrative market. It was a bold gambit that his hesitant predecessor, William McKinley, would never have made. But the warning was less risky than it appeared; it was implicitly backed by Britain (which maintained a treaty of alliance with Japan at the time). In the end, the tactic prevented a larger conflict that might have spread to Europe and beyond.

Roosevelt prevented another war in 1906, convincing a haughty French government to attend the Algeciras Conference and thereby placate Germany, which threatened war if its interests in Morocco were not recognized. Had he not intervened, France would likely not have participated, since it realized its mere presence at the conference would be a diplomatic triumph for Germany, giving de facto recognition to Kaiser Wilhelm II's dubious right to interfere in France's rule of Morocco. By persuading France to swallow its pride and go to Algeciras, TR might have prevented World War I from erupting eight years earlier than it did. Had TR not involved himself in the dispute (he could have easily done nothing), the proud and prickly German leader could have lashed out with his army, the most powerful in Europe, had he been humiliated before the eyes of the world (the strength of the Kaiser's resolve was plain to see in his decision to amass troops on the French border during the crisis).

The following year Roosevelt likely prevented a war in the Pacific between the United States and Japan, when Japan was angered by discrimination against Japanese immigrants in California. The Asian power might have used the issue as a pretext to seize the Philippines and Hawaii. Responding to the shrill, manufactured complaints coming from Japan's embassy in Washington, Roosevelt ordered the entire U.S. Navy, including all sixteen battleships then afloat, to sail into the Pacific Ocean on a "training mission." This was a forceful message to Japan's government: the United States was not afraid to fight to defend its vital interests. Japan's complaints suddenly ceased, after it was confronted by this dramatic flexing of America's naval might.

If Roosevelt was a warmonger he could have easily used any of these four volatile situations to thrust the United States into war, and yet he did the exact opposite, using his diplomatic skill to keep the United States (and other countries) out of war. The results speak for themselves, as does his Nobel Peace Prize (which he earned for brokering an end to the Russo-Japanese War) and his vigorous support for the Hague Peace Conference (he persuaded the other great powers to attend to promote international peace).

Roosevelt supported the idea of creating an international forum to resolve disputes between nations, as long as its creation was not used as an excuse to reduce the military strength of the United States. He had first floated the idea for a "League to Enforce Peace" at his 1910 speech accepting the Nobel Peace Prize, declaring: "It would be a master stroke if those Great Powers, honestly bent on peace, would form a League of Peace, not only to keep the peace among themselves, but to prevent by force if necessary its being broken by others."[17]

This was not an entirely new idea, but TR was the first major world leader to propose an international police force to give it teeth. This proposal was a natural extension of his Roosevelt Corollary to the Monroe Doctrine, which asserted the right of the United States to police the Western Hemisphere. He believed other great nations had the right to police their own "spheres of influence." So the idea of combining all these regional policing efforts into a single global body like a "League of Peace" fit perfectly into his thinking, though he refused to cede the security of the United States to such a body. It was that reservation, in addition to others, that made him question Woodrow Wilson's conception of a "League of Nations." Had TR lived beyond January 1919, these doubts would have probably made him join with his closest friend, Henry Cabot Lodge, in opposing Wilson's plan when it was debated in the U.S. Senate and ultimately rejected by that body.

A large part of Roosevelt's reputation as a warmonger is fueled by his unpopular efforts to push the United States into World War I. It is fair to criticize him during the first year of the war, when he argued unpersuasively that Germany's violation of Belgium's neutrality was reason enough to enter the conflict. But once Germany sank the *Lusita-nia* in 1915, killing more than a hundred American civilians, he could claim a legitimate *casus belli* as justification for the United States sending troops to Europe.

Lost in the portrayal of Roosevelt as a man who loved war is the real genius he showed for diplomacy. His combination of toughness and tact made him an ideal diplomat, at least when his competing traits were equally balanced. In his dealings with the other great nations, he could be persuasive and cagey, resolute and demanding. He understood the legitimate interests of foreign powers, he could recognize and even sympathize with their competing points of view, and he could assuage volatile egos (like that of Kaiser Wilhelm), while never being less than adamant in asserting American rights, as he demonstrated in refusing to give up an inch of territory to the British during the Alaskan boundary dispute. If one wanted to criticize Roosevelt's foreign policy, one would have to point to Latin America, where he reaped arguably huge rewards—building the Panama Canal, defusing crises that could have involved foreign intervention in Venezuela and Santo Domingo—but at the cost of making the United States an unpopular constabulary force in the region.

"TR WAS A MILITANT ENVIRONMENTALIST"

Theodore Roosevelt has received immense praise for elevating the conservation movement—which in the latter half of the nineteenth century was confined to small groups of naturalists, hunters, and outdoorsmen—onto the national stage and successfully persuading the American people that the country's natural resources needed to be safeguarded for abundant use by future generations.

When Americans visit a national park, monument, sanctuary, or preserve, they instantly appreciate the wisdom and foresight of TR's aggressive conservation policy. He protected 150 million acres of virgin forests from indiscriminate commercial exploitation, created the nation's first federal wildlife refuge in Pelican Island, Florida, and added fifty more by the end of his administration. However, these achievements create the impression that his conservation policy was driven solely by a desire to keep the natural wonders of the country in a pristine condition.

Roosevelt, of course, was sensitive to the beauty of places like the Grand Canyon, which he made off limits to commercial development when he declared it a national monument. But he and his chief of forestry, Gifford Pinchot, were leaders of the utilitarian branch of the conservation movement. They wanted not merely to preserve the country's forests for the sake of their beauty but also manage them so they could be replenished and used to drive the economic development of the country in a sustainable way. He wanted to keep the lumber industry away from some forests, like those along the California coast, which contained ancient and irreplaceable Sequoia trees. Other forests he considered "factories of wood" that could safely be harvested as crops of timber as long as cut-down trees were replaced by new ones.[18] His conservation policy was expressed in unmistakable terms when he convinced Congress in 1905 to transfer care of the nation's forests from the Department of Interior to the Department of Agriculture. He believed the latter was better equipped to deal with "crop management."[19]

He was also sensitive to the dangers of deforestation, bemoaning the extinction of birds like the passenger pigeon and the ivory-billed woodpecker. At the same time he wanted to make use of the country's natural resources to increase the power of the United States relative to other nations.

Given Roosevelt's utilitarian approach, he would not have seen eye-to-eye with today's environmentalists, who seem to condemn any practical use of the country's natural resources as a colossal crime. After all, he created the Reclamation Service, which by the end of the twentieth century had constructed seven hundred dams and sixteen thousand miles of aqueducts to bring water to the arid states of the West. Collectively, these projects came at a high cost to the environment. Most would be opposed in knee-jerk fashion by no-growth environmentalists were they proposed in our own time, but TR did not lose sleep over the downside to his irrigation policy. He focused on the huge boost to the nation's development that would occur if water were made available in desolate areas where it had once been impossible for people to live. He loved nature as few American presidents ever have, but he loved the American people more.

CHAPTER FOUR

THE BULL MOOSE PROGRESSIVE

~

E ver since his Bull Moose presidential candidacy of 1912, Roosevelt has been unfairly vilified by conservatives for splitting the Republican Party and, as a consequence, for putting the progressive Democrat, Woodrow Wilson, in the White House. The evidence, however, indicates that Taft would have lost to Wilson even had Roosevelt stayed on the sidelines. Roosevelt thought he had a better chance of beating Wilson than Taft did—and he was right.

Taft meant well during his forgettable administration, but he was a natural judge rather than a natural president—much better at parsing matters of law than leading—and an inept politician. His dream had been to become chief justice (a goal he later achieved), not president, of the United States. No friend of Taft, Gifford Pinchot remarked with more than a little truth: "After TR came Taft. It was as though a sharp sword had been succeeded by a roll of paper, legal size."[1]

One of Roosevelt's skills as president had been his vigorous leadership of the Republican Party and his ability to sweep both conservatives and progressives under the Republican banner. But Taft lacked that political skill. A deeply conservative man, Taft needlessly alienated progressive Republicans by signing the controversial Payne-Aldrich tariff, a failed compromise bill that split the Republican Party between its free trade and protectionist wings. The law made a pretense of lowering import duties, which the progressives supported, but essentially maintained the protective tariff that pro-business stalwarts insisted must remain in place to ensure national prosperity.

This occurred in 1909 while Roosevelt was hunting game in Africa. When he returned to the United States in June 1910, the Republican Party coalition of progressives and conservatives had collapsed. A month before TR's return, the *New York Times* wrote: "These are black days for the Republicans in Congress.... The leaders of the old [Republican] organization are in despair.... No longer is there any pretense of enacting Mr. Taft's measures on their merits as laws."[2]

In November's congressional elections, the Republican Party suffered a massive and embarrassing defeat, losing control of the House of Representatives for the first time since 1894 and retaining only tenuous control of the U.S. Senate. In contrast, under President Roosevelt the Republicans had actually gained seats in the House and Senate in the 1904 general election and in the Senate in the 1906 midterm election.

The Republican split was caused not by Roosevelt but by Taft, and talk of forming a third party had already started before Roosevelt returned to the United States in 1910. Roosevelt merely responded to the Republican divisions and Taft's general unpopularity.

If Roosevelt had not taken leadership of the Progressives, it is likely that someone else, like Senator Robert LaFollette of Wisconsin, probably would have as a third party candidate for president in 1912. Even if the rebellious progressives had not formed a new party, the overwhelming majority would not have voted for Taft in any event. As it turned out, of course, Roosevelt did run as the Progressive candidate for president in 1912, capturing 27 percent of the vote, compared to Taft's 23 percent. The real story of the 1912 election was not Roosevelt's candidacy but the overwhelming electoral support for the three candidates who ran "progressive" campaigns. Taken together, Roosevelt, Wilson, and the Socialist Eugene Debs won 75 percent of the vote that year. Even Taft, seeing the progressive mood of the voters, ran as a not very convincing progressive, making an issue of his busting more trusts in four years than TR had in eight, reveling in his decision to bring suit against U.S. Steel— a step TR had declined to take in 1907. Seen in this light, TR's decision to run in the 1912 election was a reasonable gamble, assuming he could tap into the cresting wave of progressivism and ride it all the way into the White House. Roosevelt's coalition was almost a precursor of Ronald Reagan's—crossing party lines, attracting "plain people," including Northern Catholics and Southern Protestants—and Roosevelt's insurgent campaign was a bit like Reagan's 1976 primary campaign against Gerald Ford, a sitting Republican president, though of course Reagan did not make the break to run as third party candidate. (TR's third party, the Progressive Party, was dubbed by the press "the Bull Moose Party" after TR remarked that he felt "as strong as a bull moose" when it came to the rigors of a national campaign.) One of the ironies of the 1912 election was that many of the reforms Roosevelt advocated during the campaign were eventually enacted into law by his archenemy, Woodrow Wilson.

SENSIBLE REFORMS VINDICATED BY POSTERITY

Critics of Roosevelt condemn him for his radicalism during this period; they point to his Osawatomie speech in 1910 as proof he had veered so far left that he was really a socialist. But an examination of the Bull Moose platform reveals moderation rather than radicalism at a time when the electorate seemed overwhelmingly in favor of progressive reforms.

For example, the Bull Moose Party favored a graduated income tax to replace high tariffs. Many libertarians hate the income tax, but the fact is that in 1909 a *Republican* Congress voted in favor of the Sixteenth Amendment to the Constitution, which permitted an income tax (the amendment was needed because in 1895 the Supreme Court ruled the income tax unconstitutional). The amendment won ratification by the states in early 1913, and the first income-tax law enacted by the Wilson administration was highly popular. It generated enough revenue to allow the high tariff to be lowered (and thereby reduce prices for consumers) and was only targeted at a miniscule fraction of the population (the top 0.5 percent of income earners). Roosevelt preferred an inheritance tax to an income tax, but in the end gave the measure his support. The income tax has proven to be a better revenue-generating system than the anachronistic tariff, which was inadequate to finance the dramatic growth of American power during the twentieth century.

The Bull Moose Party supported the direct election of United States senators, which we now take for granted, and which the conservative Roosevelt had once opposed. He changed his mind because he came to see the popular election of senators as a way to defeat special interests that could control a state legislature and thus control the election of a U.S. senator. In May 1912, a Democratic Congress voted in favor of the Seventeenth Amendment to the Constitution to end the election of U.S. senators by state legislatures and give this power to the people of the individual states. Within less than a year, three-quarters of the states ratified the amendment.

The Bull Moose Party favored a system of state primaries to choose presidential nominees. First used in 1912, primary elections are now a fixture of American politics. The incentive to create primaries was to supplant the corrupt, party "boss" system of politics that Roosevelt frequently crusaded against.

The Bull Moose Party led Roosevelt into supporting women's suffrage, about which he had previously been lukewarm. President Wilson, on the other hand, repeatedly refused to support woman's suffrage, fearing it would open the door to permitting blacks to vote in the South. He eventually, however, backed the idea at the end of his administration, and the woman's suffrage amendment, the nineteenth amendment, passed Congress and was ratified by the states in 1919.

Roosevelt and the Bull Moose Party were early proponents of campaign finance reform laws. Though he himself had been attacked for taking contributions from E. H. Harriman, John D. Rockefeller, and J. P. Morgan in his 1904 presidential campaign, Roosevelt decided to turn the tables on his opponents and called for new campaign-finance laws that would limit the amount of financial contributions candidates for public office could receive, and make them transparent to the public.

Roosevelt and his party also favored "social justice" laws, though these were driven not by a leftist ideology but by a social conservatism that put family life first. Proclaiming "the supreme duty of the nation is the conservation of human resources," Roosevelt pushed for regulations that are now taken for granted, including workmen's compensation, laws preventing child labor, the eight-hour work day, the six-day work week, minimum health and safety standards in the workplace, and "the family wage." But Roosevelt and his party did not, as part of its platform, support government provision of "universal healthcare." A hundred years later, President Obama, seeking to steal Republican thunder, wrongly cited "Teddy" Roosevelt as a would-be "Obamacare" supporter. Significantly, not a single notable Republican or conservative figure stood up for the historical truth, a sad commentary on their lack of knowledge and courage.

Other regulation supported by the Bull Moose Party involved government supervision of investments. Declaring "the people of the United States are swindled out of many millions of dollars every year through worthless investments,"[3] Roosevelt called for a regulatory system to protect investors—a proposal that foreshadowed the creation of the Securities and Exchange Commission after the stock market crash in 1929. In the century that followed the 1912 election, the federal government expanded the regulatory regime over the nation's financial industry. This was a good thing, especially the Glass-Steagall reforms of 1933, which separated investment from commercial banking. The near collapse of the nation's banking system in 2008, in part driven by the repeal of Glass-Steagall under President Bill Clinton, demonstrates such regulation remains needed a century after TR's Bull Moose campaign.

Similarly, the party favored currency and banking reform. After the Panic of 1907 brought the United States to the verge of economic depression, Roosevelt had a golden opportunity to push for reforms of the country's currency and banking system. He failed to do so but warmed to the idea by 1912. The Bull Moose platform accordingly denounced "the present method of issuing notes through private agencies" as "harmful and unscientific."

The party supported the idea of a national bank but opposed the Federal Reserve system (created in 1913 by the Wilson administration) because it put the "the currency and credit system in private hands" thus opening the door to "domination or manipulation by Wall Street or any special interests."

Roosevelt and his party did, however, back the creation of a Federal Trade Commission. After seeing a number of his anti-trust prosecutions fail in the federal-court system, Roosevelt concluded by the time he left the White House that the power to regulate Big Business should reside primarily within the executive branch of government, not the judiciary. In 1912, he accordingly called for setting up a new federal agency to investigate companies suspected of illegal restraint of trade under the Sherman anti-trust law. Wilson supported the idea. After entering the White House, he created the Federal Trade Commission, which continues to operate today to the benefit of American consumers and greater competition.

Foreshadowing the creation of the Interstate Highway System under Republican President Dwight Eisenhower, Roosevelt emphasized "the vital importance of good roads" during his 1912 presidential run and pledged to "foster their extension in every proper way," including "the early construction of national highways." As his successful Reclamation Service demonstrated in bringing water to portions of the arid West, he strongly favored building up the nation's infrastructure to promote commerce and development.

He was also, of course, the nation's most prominent conservationist, and the Bull Moose Progressive Party backed Roosevelt's aggressive but utilitarian approach to conserving America's natural resources. Roosevelt insisted "the natural resources of the nation must be promptly developed and generously used to supply the people's needs" while simultaneously ensuring this be done on a sustainable basis. "Conservation will not retard legitimate development," he declared in the Bull Moose Party platform.

Finally, Roosevelt was the foremost statesman for America, speaking softly but carrying a big stick in foreign affairs. The party followed his line. Pledging to promote peaceful means to settling international disputes and backing "an international agreement for the limitation of naval forces," the Bull Moose platform of 1912 also called for an expansion of the U.S. Navy by the building of two new battleships per year. Given the increased global responsibilities of the United States with the Philippines, Hawaii, and the newly constructed Panama Canal to defend, this was imperative—although modest in that the Bull Moose Party did not propose that defense spending should exceed what the government could actually afford.

Most of Roosevelt's reform agenda now seems unremarkable— indeed, to a large degree it is law. Taft, however, denounced Roosevelt as a "political neurotic" for advocating policies that would reduce the "the United States to that condition of bubbling anarchy which once characterized Latin America."[4] He was especially angered at Roosevelt's proposal that the American people be given the right to recall judicial decisions that they did not like. To establishment conservatives like Taft, this seemed like an attempt to destroy the rule of law. But Roosevelt's modest proposal applied only to the decisions of state courts (the Supreme Court and the federal courts would not be interfered with) and could only be invoked on decisions involving constitutional questions (limiting the power to only a few state-court decisions). Moreover, if there was anything Theodore Roosevelt opposed it was anarchy (and, of course, socialism).

The conservative *London Times*, the newspaper of record for the Western world at the time, was on Roosevelt's side. Tongue firmly in cheek, it mocked Taft's inability to see the bigger picture: "Alas poor England! For this power of the courts, deemed so essential to free government, is a power quite unknown to the judiciary of Great Britain. An Act of Parliament is law, whether it please the Court or no. The duty of the judiciary is confined to its interpretation and application."[5] Rushing to Roosevelt's defense and ridiculing Taft's hysteria, the *Times* added: "If to curb [judges] in their power over legislation is to violate the sacred principles of free government, of government under law, then is England, all unaware, a government without true freedom, a government not under law? For England denies to her courts entirely the power which Mr. Roosevelt advises America merely to restrain."[6]

Roosevelt's desire to give the people power to recall the judicial decisions of state courts was in line with his support for "the Initiative" (which gave citizens power to call referendums within their states), "the Referendum" (which allowed them to sidestep state legislatures and enact laws by popular vote), and "the Recall" (which allowed citizens the right, by popular vote, to chuck elected officials from office before their term expired). Senator Henry Cabot Lodge, Roosevelt's best friend but an ally of Taft in 1912, denounced the "Initiative, Referendum, and Recall" as "the most fantastic delusions with which agitators have ever attempted to mislead or perplex the public mind."[7] Yet all three procedures are practiced by many states today, as seen in the recall election that removed Governor Gray Davis of California from office and in the referenda that have legalized marijuana in Colorado and Washington. Until a narrow majority of Supreme Court justices over-ruled them, thirty-three states used popular ballot initiatives to allow "we, the people" to decide their respective state's marriage laws. Roosevelt saw "Initiative, Referendum, and Recall" as the right and duty of an American citizen, giving him power over his own government, making it a government of truly "we, the people" rather than a government (or laws) imposed upon the people.

It is telling that today's conservatives are the loudest voices demanding changes to our system of government, just as TR did a century ago. Like him, they want give the American people more power to govern themselves. Leading this charge is radio host Mark Levin, whose eleven "Liberty Amendments" read like an updated version of the Bull Moose Party's platform. Going even further than TR did in 1912, Levin wants to give Congress or the states the ability to overturn the rulings of the

Supreme Court (TR's judicial recall measure was limited to state courts only).

TR'S RELATIONSHIP WITH WOODROW WILSON

While President Wilson enacted some Bull Moose proposals, Roosevelt in his later years came to harbor strong feelings against the twenty-eighth president. "I regard Wilson with contemptuous dislike,"[8] he wrote in 1917. "His soul is rotten through and through. He hasn't a thought for the welfare of this country, or for our honor, or for anything except his own mean personal advancement."[9] He did not always condemn Wilson; the two were actually on friendly terms until the end of Roosevelt's presidency. They met sometime in the 1890s. After becoming vice president in 1901, TR invited Wilson to Sagamore Hill to discuss education in the United States. Wilson, then a leading figure in academia and interested in educational reform, glowed with enthusiasm afterwards, telling Roosevelt he "had a most delightful and refreshing time at Oyster Bay. I reached home much heartened in many ideals."[10]

A year after the visit, Wilson became president of Princeton University. Upon hearing the news, Roosevelt, now president of the United States, beamed with enthusiasm: "Woodrow Wilson is a perfect trump. I am overjoyed at his election."[11] The two men kept in touch, with Roosevelt attending the 1905 Army-Navy football game at Princeton, where he and his entourage were cordially entertained by Wilson and his wife.

The cords of friendship began to unravel, however, after Roosevelt left the White House. As long as Wilson remained on a college campus, a non-combatant in the nation's political war, no friction existed. When Wilson began to speak on national issues, plotting his own political career, their relationship changed. Using Princeton as a platform to promote himself, Wilson drew the attention of power brokers within the Democratic Party. Eager to build his partisan credentials, he began to publicly attack his old friend. He won the governorship of New Jersey in 1910.

Wilson needed political brilliance and more than a little luck to win the White House, both of which he possessed in abundance in 1912. Roosevelt, not used to being shunted to the side of the nation's political stage, was perhaps envious of the former college professor whose intellect matched his own, and whose communication and political skills were equally as strong. As the Wilson administration began in March 1913, one can picture TR sitting at home in Oyster Bay with steam blowing out of both ears. His nemesis was enjoying fanfare in pushing a sparkling array of domestic reforms through Congress, a legislative record that stands above and beyond Roosevelt's. The enactment of a new tariff, which dramatically lowered import duties and all but ended fifty years of protection, must have made TR wince; it was an issue that Roosevelt had largely avoided, seeing it as political quicksand, and to which, on its merits, he was largely indifferent, but that, under Taft, had wrecked Republican unity; and now Wilson had gone into the history books enacting historic reform.

Tariff reform at the beginning of the twentieth century makes for dry reading, but the lower tariff gave a boost to the creation of the consumer economy that eventually helped transform the United States into a super-power. Roosevelt had taken the first step in helping to build a more free-market, modern, industrial consumer economy by reviving the moribund Sherman anti-trust law, but his lukewarm trust-busting did little to reduce consumer prices. Wilson's tariff reform, however, exerted a stronger impact on the economy. It eliminated the duty on imported sugar, for example, thereby pushing prices lower by opening the door to foreign producers. The lower tariff was, in effect, a sizeable tax cut for ordinary Americans. Wilson achieved Roosevelt's goal of boosting America's consumer econ-omy, but such were the feelings of hostility between the two men that Roosevelt did not want to give him credit for it.

Neither did Roosevelt want to credit Wilson for another achieve-ment: the Federal Reserve banking system. Indeed, Roosevelt actively opposed the creation of the Federal Reserve, which had, in fact, been designed by his political enemies (like Senator Nelson Aldrich). After the Panic of 1907, the public seemed to favor currency and banking reform, yet Roosevelt had no interest in pursuing these reforms during his last year in the White House. His study of American history had convinced him that opposing a central bank was the politically safer course. As it turned out, Wilson's creation of the Federal Reserve in 1913 was widely applauded, and the praise the Wilson administration won that year as the progressive government *par excellence* poured salt in TR's political wounds. As the *Baltimore Sun* gushed:

> The President has himself disregarded all the petty restraints which heretofore hedged the Chief Executive.... He delivered a Message in person to Congress.... All this and much more he has done in three months. And as it is almost daily remarked in Washington, he has not made one single blunder. He has shown clearly the uselessness of a third party. He has obscured Theodore Roosevelt as the leader of progressivism, and has brought together the radical and conservative wings of his own party.[12]

A British newspaper, the *Daily Chronicle*, went further, declaring "no more remarkable man has reigned at the White House since Abraham Lincoln" and drawing a comparison between Wilson and his predecessor:

> Little did the people imagine that this intellectual would be able to exert so remarkable an influence over Congress and within a year of his entry into the Presidential office have succeeded in inducing the most protectionist country in the world to take so big and decisive a step in the direction of free trade.... His calm strength and definiteness of aim contrast strikingly with the boisterous energy and assertive egotism of Roosevelt. Wilson stands today before the world as a great statesman and leader of men.[13]

All this praise for Wilson's progressivism underlined something else: Roosevelt's contrasting reformist conservatism no longer seemed to capture the national mood even if it might have been better for the economy. The United States suffered a brief but deep recession in 1913, partly from the economic dislocations caused by Wilson's policies. As with his eventual Democrat successor as president, Franklin Roosevelt, it was a world war, more than progressive economic policies, that gave America's economy a boost.

For Theodore Roosevelt, it must have seemed like a good time to leave the country. So at the end of 1913, he departed on a speaking tour and bird-watching expedition that became, ad hoc, an expedition to explore the unmapped River of Doubt in South America. He nearly died during his adventure, contracting "jungle fever," and never fully recovered.

HIS LAST BATTLE

Upon his return to the United States, he grew cranky and irritable during the last five years of his life as deteriorating health added to his frustration that Wilson dominated American politics. The beginning of World War I in August 1914 gave him more reason to deride Wilson. "He has the nerve that his type so often shows in civil and domestic affairs where there is no danger of physical violence," Roosevelt said dismissively, branding his former friendly acquaintance a coward. "He will jump up and down on cheap politicians, and bully and cajole men in public life who are anxious not to part company with their political chief. But he is a ridiculous creature in international matters."[14]

Roosevelt initially supported Wilson's decision to stay out of the European conflict. After six weeks, however, he came to see Germany's violation of Belgian neutrality as an unrighteous act that merited a firm American response. While critics pointed out that TR's appeals to treaty obligations during his presidency were selective, his argument in this case gained vindication when a German U-boat sank the *Lusitania* on May 7, 1915, killing more than a thousand civilians and 128 Americans. Roosevelt believed the sacred honor of the United States was at stake and that any president worth his salt must respond promptly by urging Congress to declare war. But Wilson refused to act. Roosevelt could barely contain himself: "Think of Old Hickory letting our citizens be constantly murdered on the high seas by the Germans and in Mexico by the Greasers! But men are easily puzzled, and it is easy to mislead them, if one chooses to give them high-sounding names to excuse ignoble deeds. This is an evil service that President Wilson has rendered and is now rendering the American nation."[15]

Whatever the motivation, Wilson's decision to stay out of the war worked out well for the United States. Once the European belligerents fought themselves into a state of exhaustion during three years of horrific trench warfare, the American army entered the conflict fresh and strong. Unable to counter more than a million new soldiers flooding onto the continent to oppose it, Germany fell in less than a year. Had the United States entered the war in 1914 or 1915 as TR wanted, hundreds of thousands of American casualties might have resulted without bringing the conflict to an early conclusion.

By letting his passions loose during World War I, TR journeyed into the political wilderness, where he shouted proud and fruitless defiance. It was once said of Ty Cobb—the greatest baseball player of TR's generation—that "he would climb a mountain to punch an echo." That was Roosevelt during the final years of his life, struggling to pursue a victory he could not win. While he died peacefully in his sleep in January 1919, he was still fighting in his heart, still struggling for personal and national greatness. It was a needless battle at that late hour. Greatness for himself and the United States had already been secured thanks to his trailblazing efforts that gave Wilson success in enacting groundbreaking reforms and laid the foundation for American power in the twentieth century.

PART II

THE MAKING

OF A

CONSERVATIVE

REFORMER

1881 TO 1901

CHAPTER FIVE

TR'S POLITICAL
EDUCATION

~

W hen Theodore Roosevelt began his political career in 1881, at the age of twenty-two, he enjoyed an advantage few politicians possess when they first seek public office: name recognition. To be a Roosevelt in that time and place meant one was by default a cultured Knickerbocker aristocrat, a high-minded and upright gentleman who oozed old money and *noblesse oblige* from his pores.

The first member of the family to come to America, Klaas Martensen van Roosevelt, a Dutch immigrant, arrived in 1649 only a few decades after the landing of the *Mayflower.* Over the course of two centuries his descendants carved out a lucrative mercantile fiefdom on the island of Manhattan.

By the 1860s one of these descendants, Cornelius Van Schaack (CVS) Roosevelt (TR's grandfather), was among the ten wealthiest men in New York City as measured by his real-estate holdings, which were assessed for tax purposes at $1.3 million but probably were worth at least three times as much on the open market.

As a young man, CVS had inherited $400,000. He shrewdly invested this windfall in land and a large business that imported hardware and plate glass from Europe. A founder of Chemical Bank and an unshakeable pillar of the city's financial establishment, CVS "never failed to meet his obligations in gold."[1]

TR's father, Theodore Roosevelt Sr., was the youngest surviving son of CVS and ran the family's plate glass-import business until 1876, retiring at age thirty-five to devote his energies to philanthropic endeavors. A serious Protestant of the Dutch Reformed tradition, he used his large fortune for noble ends, supporting numerous charities.

The Roosevelts were known for their generosity, but they were first and foremost a family of hard-headed merchants who knew how to protect their financial interests. Prior to the Civil War, they put aside their opposition to slavery and supported Democrats because the party favored lowering the protective tariff that cut into the profits of the family's import business. When the South seceded in 1861, many members of the clan switched to the Republican side to support the Union cause but refused to support the party's protectionist policy.

Theodore Roosevelt Sr., a charter member of the Union League Club during the war, director of the Metropolitan Museum of Art and the American Natural History Museum, founder of New York's Orthopedic Hospital, and supporter of many other charities, was prominent enough a figure that he found himself nominated for public office. He served as commissioner of the New York State Board of Charities, but died suddenly in 1878, at age 46 (TR was 19 years old), soon after his nomination to become head of the New York Customs House was defeated in the U.S. Senate by Roscoe Conkling, the "machine boss" of the Republican Party in New York, who became a symbol to the younger Roosevelt of everything that was wrong with the American political system during the Gilded Age.

Roosevelt Sr. had been an unlikely choice for the position. He favored tariff reform, which the party stalwarts opposed, and he was a critic of the "spoils system" of granting appointments as political favors of the party machine. Yet this was one of the most important jobs in the federal government and was the party machine's to give, as Conkling proved in his successful defiance of President Rutherford Hayes. A large portion of the federal government's revenue came from import duties levied on foreign manufactured goods and raw materials entering the United States through the Port of New York; and this was a position usually given to a loyal and leading member of New York City's Republican Party machine.

TR was a student at Harvard when his father died; and his father's death changed the trajectory of his life. TR had intended to be a scientist; now he turned to politics and the vindication of his father's banner of political reform. The younger Roosevelt had no grand ideological vision, and he was certainly no left-wing ideologue or utopian. His political platform, such as he had at the time, beyond standard Republican Party positions inherited from his father (in favor of business, national development, and law and order) was focused solely on striking back at the corrupt forces that had torpedoed his father's nomination in the U.S. Senate.

TR: THE CONSERVATIVE POPULIST

Roosevelt once remarked of his early political career: "I rose like a rocket"—a fitting phrase to describe how by the age of twenty-five he had become the Republican leader in the New York Assembly (he served three one-year terms in that body from 1882 to 1884), a position usually reserved for grizzled politicians. He was propelled to prominence by a flair for the dramatic, an uncanny ability to get his name in the newspapers, and an instinctive populist touch.

Rather than sit behind his desk and vote as he was told by party bosses, Roosevelt acted as if detective work to uncover corruption was part of his job description. He hired the famous Pinkerton agency, using his own, not taxpayer, money, to investigate officeholders suspected of bad conduct.[2] His efforts convinced the New York Assembly to appoint him chairman of a special committee to investigate corruption in the public offices of New York City. Called the Roosevelt Committee, it exposed all kinds of underhanded activity on the part of government officials.

Roosevelt was driven by a sense of honesty, of righteousness, of Christian virtue and American idealism to which government corruption was an affront. But he was no unbending extremist—however fiery his rhetoric could become.

For example, Roosevelt initially supported legislation that would reduce fares on New York City's elevated railways to five cents. But the Democrat governor of New York, Grover Cleveland, thought the measure amounted to an illegal interference with private property and contract rights, and promptly vetoed the legislation as unconstitutional. Roosevelt, who had instinctively sided with the "plain people," saw the force of Cleveland's arguments, and changed his mind and took to the floor of the Assembly to deliver, per the *Chicago Tribune*, "a remarkable speech," admitting he was wrong:

> I question very seriously if the [Five Cent Fare] bill is constitutional.... I think we should not hastily pass this bill over the Governor's veto. I have to say with shame that when I voted for this bill I did not act as I think I ought to have acted.... I have to confess that I weakly yielded, partly in a vindictive spirit toward the infernal thieves and conscienceless swindlers who have the elevated railroads in charge, and partly to the popular voice of New York. For the managers of the elevated railroads I have as little feeling as any man here. If it were possible I would willingly pass a bill of attainder on Jay Gould and all of Jay Gould's associates.... I regard these men as furnishing part of that most dangerous of all dangerous orders—the wealthy criminal class.[3]

Much as he despised men who abused wealth and power, Roosevelt nevertheless supported contract and private property rights, the rule of law, and voted to uphold Cleveland's veto, not override it. He spoke like a progressive, voted like a conservative, and could best be described as a conservative populist.

He was also a political pragmatist rather than an ideologue. In June 1884, he served as a delegate representing New York at the Republican convention to select the party's presidential candidate. By this time, he had become a well-known personality within New York City; other parts of the country had begun to notice him, too, as a "young, ambitious and very wealthy" politician who had "raised the dickens with municipal abuses."[4] His participation in the 1884 convention was his official entrance into national politics, and he made a lasting first impression. Roosevelt belonged to the Mugwump faction of the party— the reform-minded, wealthy elite of the Northeast who advocated "good government." Roosevelt, the Mugwumps, and the Mugwump-friendly newspaper the *New York Times*, supported the dark horse candidacy of George Edmund, a U.S. Senator from Vermont, against the incumbent Republican President Chester A. Arthur and his most prominent rival for the nomination, James Blaine, a former U.S. Senator from Maine whose reputation was clouded with charges of corruption.

Edmund, not surprisingly, was defeated (on the fourth ballot) and the majority of the party gave its enthusiastic support to Blaine. TR loathed Blaine and had to balance that loathing with party loyalty. After he consulted with his friend Henry Cabot Lodge, he put out a statement to the press: "I intend to vote the Republican Presidential ticket.... I am by inheritance and by education a Republican. Whatever good I have been able to accomplish in public life has been accomplished through the Republican Party. I have acted with it in the past, and wish to act with it in the future."[5]

Roosevelt was pragmatic enough to support a presidential nominee he had campaigned against, something that was remembered by party powerbrokers who valued party loyalty, but he stayed true to his conscience by never actively campaigning for Blaine even as he endorsed and spoke on behalf of other Republican candidates. In the short term, though, he paid a steep political price. The high-minded Republican Mugwumps were appalled by Roosevelt's alleged ideological heresy and vilified him in the press. Without their political support, his chance of winning reelection to the New York Assembly fell dramatically.

As it was, he did not even bother to run again after his 1884 term ended. With the sudden death of his mother and his wife, he quit politics, at least for a season, to become a cowboy and cattle-rancher in the Dakota Territory.

TR: REPUBLICAN LOYALIST, TO A FAULT

When Roosevelt ran for mayor of New York City in 1886, the great political reformer ran as the approved candidate of the Republican Party machine. He was a young man, only twenty-eight, who had sown mistrust in both wings of the Republican Party—and yet here he was the Republican nominee for Mayor of New York, because while he had made important political enemies, he had also become famous and respected as a courageous reformer, cowboy statesman, and man of letters who wielded a pen as well as a rifle. He was also, in this election, something of a sacrificial lamb, because the party knew its chances of winning against the popular Democrat reformer Abram Hewitt were slim at best, and Roosevelt was nominated as the Republican alternative only weeks before Election Day.

The party machines could turn out voters within given districts and wards, which were controlled by bosses and their underlings, called "heelers" and "strikers." Votes were bought by the promise of government jobs or other financial favors. On Election Day, Roosevelt captured only 28 percent of the vote, coming in a distant third, because, aside from the popularity of the Democrat nominee, too many bosses did not trust him to be a pliable politician and too many Mugwumps thought he was too pliable given his acceptance of machine support; they did not forget his support two years earlier for James Blaine, whom they believed to be a crook.

Over the next few years Roosevelt received "a severe rib-roasting" for accepting "without protest the benefits of the usual amount of dirty work that is customary in all campaigns" when he ran for mayor in 1886.[6] One city newspaper, the *New York Star*, wrote:

> There was about the Roosevelt candidacy an atmosphere of humbug, bumptiousness, and supreme, idiotic conceit that has been absent from other Republican contentions for that high office.... Our fault with Roosevelt is not that he is wrong in his professions of devotion to the high ideal of government, but that he never practices what he preaches, and that for several years back he has, under pretense of superior patriotism and virtue, done work that the least scrupulous ward "striker" would shrink from undertaking.[7]

TR PROMOTES TARIFF REFORM, THEN BECOMES A PROTECTIONIST

Nothing reveals Roosevelt's pragmatism more than his position regarding the protective tariff, which he initially opposed and then changed his mind about. His reasons for opposing the tariff were personal. His merchant family had for generations opposed the high import duties as an unjust tax levied on their glass-importation business. Roosevelt's father had thus been an enthusiastic free trader and card-carrying member of the Cobden Club, an influential free-trade advocacy group that sought to lower tariff duties to the minimal level necessary to fund the operations of government.

Early in his career, TR had followed his father's example and dutifully joined the Cobden Club as an enthusiastic supporter of free trade. He publicly advanced the usual arguments against the protective tariff: it was an unfair tax on merchants; it helped breed corruption in the nation's ports; and it raised prices for American consumers. He stressed the injustice of the protective tariff to the larger community. It was a brave position to take for a politician wishing to rise within the Republican Party, which stood firmly committed to protection—a policy ardently advocated by the nation's conservative party since Alexander Hamilton first championed it in the 1790s.

Roosevelt knew the risks of standing upon principle as a free trader. In 1883 he wrote that "he had been warned by two or three good friends that it would be his political death if he publicly committed himself in favor of free trade."[8] However, he experienced a dramatic change of heart sometime during 1884, when he realized a future within Republican ranks would require passing all of the party's critical litmus tests. Among these, first and foremost was the requirement that year that he support James Blaine, who, however unsavory, was nonetheless the party's standard-bearer in the presidential election. Next came adherence to the protective tariff, the foundation of the party's domestic policy and the source of its political strength.

So to maintain his political viability, Roosevelt abandoned his free-trade position and resigned his membership in the Cobden Club. This sudden about-face made him acceptable as the Republican Party's candidate for mayor of New York; even so, doubts lingered about his stand on the issue. After one Republican delegate at the party's nominating convention accused TR of being a free trader, Chauncey Depew, a leading power broker in the party, chimed in to reassure the pro-protection audience that Roosevelt "has the rare courage to acknowledge that he has recovered from the errors of his youth. I suppose that when he went out of college he may have joined the Cobden Club.... He may even have had doubts of orthodox religion, but he today stands cured."[9]

TR DEFIES A PRESIDENT TO ENFORCE THE LAW

Civil service reform was one of the hottest political topics of the Gilded Age. As the federal government steadily grew, the spoils system grew with it, as each administration from Andrew Jackson onward rewarded their political supporters with government jobs. After the Civil War, the Republican Party became an unabashed champion of political patronage, using government jobs to fuel political machines in major cities across the country.

The spoils system received a mortal blow in 1883 when President James Garfield was assassinated by a "disappointed office seeker." Public opinion swung like a political sledgehammer against the spoils system, blaming it for the tragedy. Responding to this wave of indignation, Congress soon passed a law, the Pendleton Act, which provided that some government jobs would henceforth be given out on the basis of competitive examination.

Roosevelt had ardently supported the Pendleton Act, but feared it would fail through lack of enforcement, and warned that its passage was only the first battle in what would be a long war against the patronage system. That system had, in fact, helped put President Benjamin Harrison in office, as the Republican machine had turned out on his behalf. Against his better judgment, President Harrison appointed Roosevelt to the U.S. Civil Service Commission in early 1889. Harrison hoped the appointment would appease the Mugwumps, and that Roosevelt's party loyalty would, in the end, be stronger than his strident speeches and reformist zeal.

The decision backfired, however, when Roosevelt demanded the Pendleton Act be thoroughly enforced and that its flaws be amended. One such flaw was a loophole that allowed political contributions to be drawn from the wages of government workers. Called assessments, the shakedown of federal employees amounted to a vast campaign finance operation, as those who received their job through political patronage were forced to hand over 10 percent of their income as a tithe to the party.

President Harrison's reelection campaign in 1892 would be paid for by these assessments; he was understandably reluctant to see this source of financing cut at a critical moment. Roosevelt told Harrison that the Pendleton Act was not sufficient because it did nothing "to prevent political agents from seeking out government employees at their homes and bringing pressure to bear upon them there,"[10] but the president refused to help support new legislation. Tensions immediately rose between the two men, with TR remembering years later, "I got on Harrison's nerves, and whenever I came into the room he set his fingers drumming on the desk before him as though it were a piano."[11]

With the 1892 election rapidly approaching, President Harrison became less and less willing to support the reform work of the Civil Service Commission. When Roosevelt recommended that he remove the postmaster of Baltimore for non-compliance with the law, the president refused and instead sided with the postmaster general, John Wanamaker, who was the principle spoils-man within the administration and one of the most powerful members of the Cabinet. Undeterred, Roosevelt refused to quietly drop the matter. When Congress became interested, he eagerly testified before the committee investigating why the president had refused his recommendation.

Roosevelt tried to maintain a dignified public front as this ugly internecine fight within the party unfolded; in private he was infuriated by Harrison's cynical acquiescence to obvious corruption. Pouring out his rage to Henry Cabot Lodge, he boasted: "I have made this Commission a living force, and in consequence the outcry among the spoilsmen has become furious."[12] Denouncing Harrison as "a genial little runt"[13] and a "little gray, cold-blooded toad,"[14] he complained, "the President has never given us one ounce of real backing."[15] Working himself up into a crescendo of abuse, he exploded: "Damn the President! He is a cold-blooded, narrow minded, prejudiced, obstinate, timid old psalm-singing Indianapolis politician."[16] Years later in retirement, Harrison said of Roosevelt: "The only trouble I ever had with managing him was the way he wanted to put an end to all the evil in the world between sunrise and sunset."[17]

Roosevelt lost numerous bureaucratic battles, but on the whole won the war. As the *New York Times* wrote in a laudatory editorial in 1895: "It is no exaggeration to say that the cause of the emancipation of American politics from the corrupt influence of the spoils practice has been more advanced and has gained more solid ground from the work of Mr. Roosevelt during these six years than from the efforts of any other man."[18] These words were a fitting tribute to what was arguably the greatest achievement of TR's pre-presidential career, namely, his success leading the fight to rid the nation of a political pestilence that was a severe drag on the nation's development for over half a century.

TR DEFIES PUBLIC OPINION TO ENFORCE THE LAW

When he turned thirty-six at the end of 1894, Theodore Roosevelt had become one of the nation's most respected reformers fighting corruption. The American people liked him, but his political prospects were dim while party bosses controlled elections. His good fortune seemed to have run out until Mayor William Strong of New York City asked him to head the Police Board. After some hesitation, driven by a reluctance to leave national politics, he accepted the offer, seeing it as an opportunity to fight the corruption that fueled the Democrats' political machine, Tammany Hall, in his hometown.

Roosevelt won favor in the press and popular acclaim for walking the streets at night and surprising police officers who were sleeping on the job. What was less popular was his enforcement of the Raines law, which forbade the sale of alcohol on Sundays. This law had been on the books for many years yet was ignored by many of the city's saloons, especially those under the protection of Tammany Hall. Because Tammany controlled the city's police force, it was able to grant informal exemptions from the law in return for lucrative financial kickbacks from the saloons.

By enforcing the alcohol law, Roosevelt launched a political war against the Democratic Party, attacking its Mafia-like protection racket. This helped improve his standing among Republicans but angered thousands of citizens who did not care about political questions; they merely wanted to drink beer on Sundays. The city's large German community was incensed; it brewed much of the beer and no sales on Sundays decreased profits.

Smarting from the blow Roosevelt inflicted upon them, the Democrats tapped into this popular backlash; their newspaper mouthpieces soon denounced TR as a seventeenth-century Puritan trying to punish the city's sinners. Almost every New York City newspaper opposed Roosevelt because they received ads from "the gardens," "restaurants," and even brothels that served alcohol. The *Washington Post*, the paper that had been his fiercest press critic while he was a U.S. Civil Service commissioner, fired a full-broadside, writing:

> It would have been better, perhaps, if the execution of the New York Sunday law had been confided to someone less bumptious and headstrong than Roosevelt.... He is conceited to the point of bursting, and opinionated beyond the resources of descriptive writing. Having played schoolmaster here in Washington so long, he has come to regard himself as the only oracle on Earth.... Mr. Roosevelt, in a word, assumes the right of telling us what is vital and what is unimportant, and then dragoons us into a morality of his own creation.[19]

Roosevelt took these blows with aplomb and fired back at the Democrats without let-up, creating a political war that engrossed both the city and the nation. As a result, his celebrity soared to new heights. Beginning in mid-1895, cartoon images of him began to flourish and the press started calling him "Teddy," marking the beginning of his transformation from an aristocratic government official named Theodore into a man of the people. There were other telltale signs he had captured the popular imagination. In the beginning of his career, he had been scoffed at by his father's enemy Roscoe Conkling, the Republican machine boss in New York during the 1870s, as a "dentificial young man with more teeth than brains."[20] Now those big teeth, a boon to editorial cartoonists, helped him stand out among the herd of politicians.

Roosevelt boosted his career during his years in Washington as a maverick civil-service reformer, but the war against political patronage was dull compared to leading the nation's largest police force, a job that was better suited to resonate with the public's imagination. In this role he seemed like a rugged law-and-order sheriff of the Old West, cleaning up an out-of-control frontier town like Dodge City or Tombstone governed by desperadoes—fittingly, in a political war waged over saloons.

CHAPTER SIX

TR'S RUN-UP
TO THE WHITE
HOUSE

~

A fter a two-year absence, Theodore Roosevelt returned to Washington in April 1897 and entered upon the most dramatic and tumultuous period of his life when he was appointed assistant secretary of the navy by President McKinley. Up until this point, his career had been in the domestic arena; now he was in position to directly influence the government's policy toward the wider world. He had spent years fighting domestic political corruption, but international politics—and preparing the United States to assume its place with other great powers of the world—had become an abiding interest.

Roosevelt especially wanted to send a message of national strength to the fast-rising powers of Germany and Japan, and to a lesser extent Britain, America's mother country and widely regarded as the most powerful nation in the world because of its vast colonial empire and gigantic navy, but already showing signs of decline. He realized these rivals would never respect the United States unless it was first dominant within its own sphere of influence, the Western Hemisphere. He accordingly became a leading proponent of the Monroe Doctrine, urging a rapid expansion of the U.S. Navy so that the doctrine would have teeth. In private, his position was even more forceful, telling confidantes he wanted to drive every European power out of the Western Hemisphere. This was an extreme position. Britain, certainly, would not easily be dislodged from Canada. Spain on the other hand, had already lost most of its colonial possessions in the new world, had not been a great power for a century, and its hold on Cuba was shaky after revolution erupted on the island in 1895. Cuba, less than a hundred miles off the coast of Florida, had always been of interest to the United States, including as a possible future possession. Roosevelt and others saw an opportunity to create a colonial empire that would increase American power and bring peace and stability to the island; TR and his allies lobbied for American intervention in Cuba's internal war.

President Grover Cleveland had used diplomatic notes to protest Spain's oppressive policy in Cuba, and the McKinley administration did the same. But neither administration was prepared to go beyond heated rhetoric. Roosevelt supported a more aggressive approach, but the American people did not. That changed, however, in February 1898, when the battleship *Maine* exploded and sank in Havana harbor (it had been sent to Cuba to protect Americans from Cuban riots). "The *Maine* was sunk by an act of dirty treachery on the part of the Spaniards I believe,"[1] Roosevelt declared when he heard the news. He was enraged at the loss of American life but also considered the situation a *casus belli* thrust into the nation's lap that promised to land America a colonial empire. It might also give him the opportunity to fulfill his lifelong dream to risk life and limb in battle.

He attempted to persuade President McKinley to seize Cuba immediately, yet the cautious president would not act with haste. But when the Navy's investigation into the sinking was completed in April 1898, and reported that the *Maine* had been sunk due to an external explosion, likely a mine, it unleashed a wave of public anger that McKinley could not contain. The president gave Spain an ultimatum: grant Cuba independence or face war against the United States. When Spain refused, Congress promptly declared war by a nearly unanimous vote.

Looking on the crisis from a century removed from the passions of the moment, Roosevelt was absolutely right in demanding a tougher policy toward Spain; he stood on less firm ground demanding an armed intervention in Cuba merely because it oppressed its people. Other European powers, after all, exploited the inhabitants of their colonies all over the world, especially in Africa, where foreign rule was often brutal. Such exploitation, however, was seen by many, including Roosevelt, as abuses of an otherwise beneficent system of colonialism that, where practiced correctly, was assumed to be a praiseworthy effort to lift savage peoples up to the level of the civilized world by building roads and ports, providing medical services and education, as well as the rule of law, and creating a network of international trade.

Moreover, because Spain's culpability in the sinking of the *Maine* was not definitively proven by the official investigation, the United States did not have a legitimate reason to declare war. It did so because the American people were whipped into a frenzy by the sensationalist yellow press, led by the *New York World* and the *New York Journal*, owned by Joseph Pulitzer and William Randolph Hearst. From the perspective of abstract morality, McKinley was right to try to avoid war. Roosevelt's hawkish view, however, was the right position given realpolitik. Unrest in Cuba was a potential national security interest of the United States and flexing American muscle would, in Roosevelt's view, have a great impact in demonstrating American power to defend the Monroe Doctrine. The "splendid little war" against Spain, as Secretary of State John Hay famously described it, had the practical effect of creating the American colonial empire that Roosevelt desired. At the conclusion of the conflict, that empire included Cuba, Puerto Rico, the Philippines, and Hawaii (which was annexed as a wartime necessity) added onto the country's continental territory.

All of this might still have happened had Roosevelt not been assistant secretary of the navy, but it is undeniable that he was the most aggressive force within the administration arguing for and preparing the U.S. Navy for the coming war against Spain. The contest was, in fact, largely a naval struggle, decided when American fleets overwhelmed Spanish warships in Cuba and the Philippines. He was not present for these victories but his leadership assured the outcome. He successfully lobbied to place Admiral George Dewey as commander of the U.S. fleet in the western Pacific. Dewey became a hero when he seized Manila soon after war was declared, an action prompted by Roosevelt, who sent a telegram before hostilities began instructing him to seize the Philippines if the U.S. declared war on Spain.

Americans remember most of all Roosevelt's charge up Kettle Hill in Cuba (San Juan was the name of the larger ridge that was assaulted). It was a cinematic moment, vividly depicted in Frederic Remington's painting of the scene, that epitomizes TR's valor and patriotism more than anything else he ever did. Demonstrating incredible courage by hurling himself into a wave of Spanish rifle fire, he miraculously survived and eventually won the Congressional Medal of Honor for his heroics.

GOVERNOR ROOSEVELT

Roosevelt returned from Cuba a national hero, and newspapers were soon promoting him as a potential gubernatorial candidate in New York, where an election was only months away. The newspapers declared Roosevelt the perfect man for the job and the perfect man to remove the taint of corruption that had fallen over the state's Republican Party.

The incumbent Republican governor Frank Black was seen as a likely loser if he were to run for reelection, but GOP boss Thomas C. Platt (known as "Easy Boss") wanted to give Black, his handpicked man, another term in Albany. The party's image within the states as an engine of corruption made that impossible, so he was stuck with the Rough Rider. Roosevelt, he knew, would refuse to take orders but he was preferable to a Democrat. Platt's misgivings were somewhat assuaged when Roosevelt made a public visit to Manhattan to solicit Platt's support.

Roosevelt never made any promises to Platt about how he would govern the state, promising only to consult with Platt on a weekly basis. Roosevelt was proud, and Platt was rueful, that Governor Roosevelt did whatever he pleased, regardless of Platt's wishes.

But the mere sight of his meeting with a man who epitomized the boss system of political corruption made him appear to be more of a party hack than an idealistic reformer. For Roosevelt, it was another matter of pragmatism. He would not take orders from Platt, but he still needed his support and the votes Platt could deliver. Roosevelt knew the governorship of New York could be his stepping stone to the White House, just as it had been for Grover Cleveland in 1884. Riding a wave of popularity as a war hero and pushed forward by Platt's blessing, Roosevelt appeared to be poised for an easy victory in the November 1898 gubernatorial election, yet ended up winning by a margin of just eighteen thousand votes. His narrow victory was attributable to the weakness of the Republican Party in the state, thanks to a political scandal about management of the Erie Canal, and to a lack of enthusiastic support from both the party's machine, which always distrusted him, and even more important the reformers who wanted him to run as an independent, entirely removed from party corruption.

All this highlighted that his obvious strengths as a candidate were matched by obvious weaknesses. He was called a tax dodger by his enemies for moving to Washington to avoid paying property taxes in New York, a charge that he tacitly admitted when he paid the back taxes he owed. Many of the alcohol-imbibing citizens of the state never forgave him for his straitlaced conduct as police commissioner of New York City enforcing the Raines law, with many of his detractors believing he was a puritanical dictator who, as one of his critics opined in the campaign, "wishes to take away the poor man's pleasures."[2]

TR: THE CONSERVATIVE REFORMER

Never permitting his genteel pedigree to hinder his ambitions, Roosevelt the aristocrat wanted to be the voice of the common people—and he also wanted to dissuade the common people from following the populist leftism of the likes of William Jennings Bryan; he wanted to prove that conservatives could be reformers too. As governor of New York, he burnished his progressive credentials as a reformer, while continuing, on

public stages, to advocate an aggressive colonial policy that favored governing the recently acquired Spanish territories of the Philippines, Cuba, and
Puerto Rico—and with a firm hand when necessary (the anti-colonialist
Bryan wanted to give the Philippines independence immediately). In 1899,
when Philippine insurrectionists seemed to be gaining strength, he advised
President McKinley to send more troops, which in today's parlance would
be called a "surge" strategy.

The most powerful progressive thrust Roosevelt initiated as governor
was the franchise tax, which he pushed through the state's legislature.
The tax was imposed on public utilities like gas companies and street
railways; he said it was intended to relieve the "improper and excessive
portion of the general taxes" paid by "the farmers, the market gardeners,
and the mechanics and tradesmen" of the state. While defending the
businessmen who fueled the state's economic engine, he declared "a
corporation which derives its powers from the state should pay to the
state a just percentage of its earnings as a return for the privileges it
enjoys."[3]

Although Roosevelt's new tax was modest, relative to today's standards, it was revolutionary for its day, with one newspaper calling it "the
most radical departure in tax legislation the state has ever known."[4] More
important, it established a political stance that would continue into his
presidency: enacting policies over the organized leadership of his own
party but with the support of Democrats. Calculating that the anger he
generated among machine Republicans would be more than offset by his
increased popularity among the people, he created a tax system that
increased "the revenue of New York City alone by a good $15,000,000
yearly," which was enough money "to build a new Brooklyn Bridge every
year, or a rapid transit tunnel in less than three years, or public schools
for 10,000 children yearly."[5]

If Roosevelt's long-term goal was the White House, such progressive policies would likely prove popular with a national electorate—
though he had no ambition to run in 1900, with President McKinley
certain to secure the party's nomination to run for a second term. Nor
did he, initially, seem to have much interest in being second on the

ticket, a position that had suddenly opened up with the death of Vice President Garrett Hobart.

Roosevelt told his friend Leonard Wood that the vice presidency was "an utterly anomalous office, one which I think ought to be abolished." He nonetheless admitted, "the man who occupies it may at any moment be everything"[6] if the president were to suddenly die, as had happened when the presidency was assumed by vice presidents John Tyler, Millard Fillmore, Andrew Johnson, and Chester Alan Arthur. If he was on the fence about seeking the job, the omnipresent Henry Cabot Lodge— among the shrewdest political advisors in American history—succeeded in "badgering" him to not let the golden opportunity slip away.[7]

Having observed the failures of ambitious men like Admiral George Dewey and Thomas "Czar" Reed to win the Republican nomination because they loudly announced their desire to receive it, Roosevelt took the opposite approach: he played coy. Roosevelt made announcements from Albany that he did not want the vice president's job and would refuse the nomination if he received it, even though no one had queried him about the matter.

Roosevelt's old enemies at the *Washington Post* realized his intentions, and wrote a scathing editorial under the headline "A Surplus of Declinature," which noted "hardly a week has passed since the inauguration of Governor Roosevelt but a dispatch under an Albany date line has informed an anxious country that under no circumstances conceivable would he permit himself to be stored away in the Vice Presidency.... The *Post* cannot but sympathize with Roosevelt in his efforts to secure seclusion and avoid publicity."[8]

Governor Roosevelt attended the Republican National Convention at Philadelphia in 1900 wearing his Rough Rider campaign hat, which attracted attention, even if its real purpose was to hide a gash, bump, and shaved spot on his head—the gash and the bump received while romping with his children. He declared he was attending "merely as a spectator in order to put a check upon the scheme to nominate him,"[9] which, ironically, made the convention delegates want to nominate him even more. Perhaps equally ironically, TR's antagonistic relationship with

GOP boss Thomas Platt helped him secure the vice presidency. Exasperated by the progressive policies Roosevelt had pursued in governing New York, especially the franchise tax, Platt was eager to remove the "bloody anarchist"[10] from his sight. Conspiring with other Republican bosses, he ginned up support for Roosevelt at the convention and thereby derailed Mark Hanna's effort to choose a safe, non-progressive candidate to run alongside McKinley.

President McKinley was a popular president in 1900 and likely would have breezed to reelection without Roosevelt's help, but the reform-minded governor of New York proved an ideal running mate, providing ideological balance that helped defuse the left's stinging critique of McKinley as a pawn of Wall Street. Roosevelt also provided geographic balance to the ticket as he was popular in the Northeast and the West, which provided incremental strength to McKinley's political base in the Midwest (his home state was Ohio). Though McKinley could have followed the advice of his campaign manager, Mark Hanna, and blocked Roosevelt's nomination, he agreed to the decision of the convention; TR as vice president, he thought, made good political sense.

PART III

TR AS

PRESIDENT:

DOMESTIC

POLICY

1901 TO 1909

≈

CHAPTER SEVEN

THE TRUST-
BUSTER MYTH

∼

Theodore Roosevelt is remembered as the Trust Buster, who at the beginning of the last century waged war against monopolistic corporations, breaking them up in order to protect American consumers from ravenous captains of industry who were intent on stifling competition and amassing mountains of wealth for themselves. While this legendary portrait of a hero standing alone against an army of greedy Robber Barons makes a compelling story, it is largely a myth. TR's policy toward the trusts was more complicated than the Trust Buster slogan suggests. By the end of his presidency, TR was more a Trust Regulator than anything else, desirous that "good trusts," as he called large corporations that complied with the law, be encouraged to promote the nation's economic growth under what would later become the Federal Trade Commission.

To understand the story of Roosevelt and the trusts, we need to see his attitudes and actions in context. During the generation that preceded his presidency, the United States underwent a tremendous transformation, with the industrial revolution wrenching the country out of its agricultural past and thrusting it suddenly into an unstable present where many Americans lived in densely populated cities rather than on isolated farms. Rapid change in the way people lived created new problems that soon found an outlet in legitimate public complaints about the poor quality of life for those on the lower rungs of society.

Industrial magnates and Wall Street financiers had become remarkably wealthy, and the growing but still relatively small middle class was well off, but the laboring masses, working for low wages in jobs that were often hazardous to their health, looked on in envy and discontent. Eager to break the chains of "industrial slavery," as the liberal economist and reformer Henry George put it (George had been Roosevelt's United Labor Party opponent in the 1886 New York City mayoralty campaign),[1] labor agitators, anarchists, and socialists sometimes resorted to violence in an attempt to change the social order.

While public opinion largely condemned the labor agitators who disturbed the tranquility of the Gilded Age, the American people as a whole began to sympathize with the anger that leftist extremists vented toward the country's super-rich. Instead of taking steps to blunt "the ugly force that seethes beneath the social crust,"[2] Roosevelt warned, the rich flaunted their wealth. As a consequence, public opinion turned against the industrial magnates and Wall Street financiers, and was channeled by leftist firebrands against the monopolistic trusts, the money-making machines for the wealthiest rung of society.

REPUBLICAN RESISTANCE TO REFORMING THE TRUSTS

The trusts that flourished at end of the nineteenth century were national corporations created with the goal of dominating various sectors of the economy by eliminating competition, giving consumers no alternative to the trust's products and services, which of course increased sales and boosted profits. Monopolies are illegal today, but in the post–Civil War era they operated without restriction. Given this situation, Roosevelt had ample justification for wanting to impose new regulations that broke up monopolies, increased competition, and protected workers and consumers.

John D. Rockefeller's Standard Oil Company was the first trust to capture the public's attention. Organized in 1870, it soon controlled more than 90 percent of domestic oil refining, and came to epitomize the ruthless, piratical methods used by Big Business. Seeing the success of Rockefeller's business model, like-minded businessmen adopted the same approach. In short order, the Whisky Trust, the Sugar Trust, the Tobacco Trust, and many others were created; nearly every sector of the American economy was dominated by a single, monopolistic corporation by the end of the nineteenth century.

It took twenty years for the federal government to take action, passing the Sherman Anti-Trust Act in 1890, making it illegal for corporations to intentionally restrain competition for their own advantage. While a step in the right direction, the law was passed more to placate public opinion than to prevent monopolistic abuses. The Republican Congress that passed the act, and the Republican president who signed it into law, Benjamin Harrison, could hardly be called progressive-minded reformers; the Republicans were the party of Big Business. Indeed, the same year they passed the McKinley tariff, which imposed the highest duties on imported manufactured goods and raw materials in American history. Protected by this insurmountable tariff wall, the ultimate restraint of trade, the trusts had no fear of inexpensive imports undercutting their monopolistic schemes.

Over the next decade, the political class became complicit by ignoring the trust problem. In his last two years in office, President Harrison did little or nothing to ensure that the Sherman Anti-Trust Act was enforced, and his complacent attitude was matched by that of his Democrat successor, Grover Cleveland. The Democrats had an influential wing that behaved as the Republican stalwarts did, supporting the gold standard, the status quo, and the trusts. Cleveland was one of these "Gold Democrats" (he could have never reached the White House had he not been) and in conjunction with his ultra-conservative attorney general, Richard Olney, refused to enforce the Sherman Act in a mean-ingful way.

The Supreme Court agreed with Cleveland and Olney. In the famous 1895 *United States v. E. C. Knight* case involving a suit brought against the Sugar Trust, the Court ruled that the Constitution only gave the federal government the power to act against trusts engaged in interstate commerce, and that the Sherman Act therefore could not be used against trusts operating within a given state.

The Knight ruling helped the trusts in the short term; in the long run it accelerated the shift of public opinion against them. The American people had been lulled to sleep by the passage of the Sherman Act in 1890, believing the problem had been addressed. Once the Supreme Court announced itself the champion of the trusts, indignation grew anew. In the 1896 presidential contest, William Jennings Bryan seized on the altered public mood and made the anti-trust issue a centerpiece of his campaign. The ideological opposite of the "Gold Democrat" Grover Cleveland, Bryan promised to take on the trusts in a way no president had up to that point, including prosecuting industrial barons like John D. Rockefeller with the goal of landing them in federal prison as white-collar criminals.

Wall Street bankers and trust magnates poured millions of dollars into McKinley's campaign to persuade voters that Bryan was a dangerous radical, and while McKinley won, Bryan's pledge to take on the trusts remained popular with the public.

It was against this backdrop that Theodore Roosevelt began to take an interest in anti-trust policy. Throughout the 1890s, he barely mentioned the issue in his private correspondence and public speeches. He was concerned with eliminating the spoils system, reforming the New York City Police Department, and expelling Spain from Cuba. But after he was elected governor of New York in November 1898 and his career track shifted away from executive appointments to elective office, he came to see the country's anti-trust problem as a golden political opportunity.

He had not forgotten the tidal wave of popular support that erupted after William Jennings Bryan delivered his electrifying "Cross of Gold" speech at the Democratic Party's 1896 convention, nor the surprising showing of the economic reformer Henry George in the 1886 New York City mayoral election a decade earlier. He believed he could tap into this reformist popular sentiment, while diverting it from radical or socialist programs. So in August 1899, he set his mind on learning everything he could about an economic issue he had ignored, writing to a friend who was knowledgeable about the subject:

> How about trusts? I know this is a very large question, but more and more it seems to me that there will be a good deal of importance to the trust matter in the next campaign and I want to consult with men whom I trust most as to what line of policy should be pursued. During the last few months I have been exceedingly alarmed at the growth of the popular unrest and popular distrust on this question. It is largely aimless and baseless, but there is a very unpleasant side to this over-run trust development and what I fear is, if we do not have some consistent policy to advocate then the multitudes will follow the crank who advocates the absurd policy, but who does advocate something.[3]

This snapshot of Roosevelt's early thinking reveals his instinctive conservatism, his natural Republican support for business (dismissing most "popular distrust" of trusts as "baseless"), and his interest in tapping into popular sentiment and diverting potentially dangerous radicalism through prudent reform.

Governor Roosevelt delivered his first major speech on the trusts in his Message to the New York legislature in January 1900. He proclaimed that while the trusts committed "occasional wrongs," "the large majority of the fortunes that now exist in this country have been amassed, not by injuring mankind, but as an incident to the conferring of great benefits on the community,"[4] and that anti-trust laws should in no way "attempt to limit and hamper the acquisition and output of wealth."[5] The intellectual father of free-market capitalism, Adam Smith, couldn't have said it better.

Concluding his speech, however, Roosevelt declared the foundation of his attitude toward the trusts for the remainder of his life: that government had a "right to interfere" in their operations for the public good in the same manner in which the government regulates banks.[6] Accordingly, he advocated legislation that would create trust examiners to inspect the books and workings of corporations, just as bank examiners did to keep financiers honest. The speech generated little news, with the *New York Times* branding it "barren of positive recommendations," and observing, "Governor Roosevelt lacks the ability to think out a social and economic problem to a clearly reasoned and definite conclusion."[7]

When Roosevelt became president, he boldly shifted the Republican Party in a more populist direction without abandoning the party's platform of supporting the gold standard and the protective tariff. He did so by rigorously enforcing the Sherman anti-trust law against a handful of monopolistic corporations, creating an object lesson in reform without disrupting the American economy.

PICKING A FIGHT WITH J. P. MORGAN

Roosevelt hoped to show the American people he was on their side, that he was a Trust Buster as passionately devoted to their interests as the populist William Jennings Bryan, but one who knew how to achieve reform without dangerous revolution that would destroy an otherwise healthy American economy. TR picked a fight with the man recognized as the paramount leader of the Gilded Age plutocracy—the country's most powerful financier, J. P. Morgan.

This was a risky move—even if it proved an immensely popular one. Trust magnates and Wall Street financiers were the financial backbone of the Republican Party. They had put McKinley in the White House in 1896 and 1900 through their generous campaign contributions to stop Bryan. Most politicians in Roosevelt's place would have decided to adhere to the time-tested dictum, "Don't bite the hand that feeds you." But Roosevelt's keen political sense and natural crusading spirit put him on a different course.

While Roosevelt knew initiating a war with J. P. Morgan and his allies seemed like madness to denizens of the Union League Club, he perceived that Morgan was the ideal villain—infamous for the way he dominated the financial world and the leader of the "money power" that was seemingly indifferent to the needs of ordinary people.

In April 1901, a newspaper headline blared "Octopus Gigantic: The Trust of all Trusts Planned,"[8] announcing the news that Morgan was about to create a new combination by joining together the Northern Pacific and Great Northern railroads, creating the second biggest corporation in the world after U.S. Steel.[9]

Roosevelt—who became president in September 1901—struck his decisive blow in February 1902, when he announced his Justice Department had begun legal proceedings against J. P. Morgan's Northern Securities company with the goal of dissolving the combination as an illegal "restraint of trade" under the Sherman anti-trust law. The news shook Wall Street like an earthquake, with the market capitalization of Morgan's railroad combination, valued at $400 million when formed, losing one-eighth of its value (or $55 million) in a single day.[10] Upon hearing about the president's bold action, a prominent financier allied with the Morgan interests observed: "The business of the country appears to be conducted at Washington now."[11]

Once the initial shock of Roosevelt's anti-trust action subsided, Wall Street's fears eased. The federal courts were the final arbiter that would decide the fate of the Northern Securities holding company, not the president, and the judges who sat on the federal bench had shown a distinct bias in favor of Big Business. Trust-busting might be politically popular, but it seemed almost certain it would be overturned by the courts.

Whatever the courts did, even the Republican Party was coming to recognize that Roosevelt had landed a political masterstroke. Roosevelt's old friend Chauncey Depew, Republican senator from New York, declared Roosevelt's "stock is going up with the people every day."[12]

As the Republican Party adjusted to the apparent reversal of its pro-business policy and the growing popularity of its reform-minded leader, the Democrats shook their heads in disbelief; their crusade against the trusts had suddenly been taken up by a Republican president. Not surprisingly, they saw a political motive behind his policy, with Democrat congressman Francis Newlands pointing out: "The President did not become imbued with this anti-trust hunting idea until the Democrats had adopted it as their leading issue. After seven months of silence on the subject, he has suddenly discovered that it is a burning question."[13] "From a Democratic view," said an equally miffed member of the opposition party, President Roosevelt was "a weird magician of politics."[14]

While the Democrats were mystified at how the tables had been turned against them, Wall Street reacted with predictable anger when it learned the Republican Party was no longer in its pocket. Refusing to accept the change with quiet grace, J. P. Morgan and his allies used the newspapers and journals they controlled to unleash a barrage of criticism against Roosevelt, including a scathing attack in *Harper's Weekly* in response to an anti-trust speech the president gave in Wheeling, West Virginia, in September 1902:

> The daily newspapers in their headlines announced that the President had gone a step forward in his war on combinations, but a reading of the speech did not confirm the headlines. The truth is that the President has not uttered a single statesman-like word on the subject. He has dealt in the vaguest kind of generalities. He speaks of evils without specifying them, and has even seemed to admit that the ills he denounces with his customary vigor are yet to be discovered.... When a statesman who occupies the most responsible, as well as the most conspicuous position in the country, enters upon the discussion of proposed reforms, it is his duty to particularize, to present details, to give his reasons, and to unfold his argument and plan.... His speeches have been as those of one who is talking merely for political effect, and for the purpose, quite unworthy of such a man as Theodore Roosevelt, of stealing the enemy's thunder, and of putting the Democrats in a hole.[15]

TR CHAMPIONS THE ELKINS ACT

This Wall Street-inspired critique fails to provide a full account of TR's motives. He certainly yearned for a second term, and political expediency undoubtedly was a factor driving his policy. Yet the president was legitimately worried about the growing socialist movement, which he feared might become "a great movement in the country at large of a very formidable character" and compel the government to "take possession of the railroads."[16] By taking on the trusts, he rightfully believed he would take the steam out of this movement on the extreme left.

He brushed aside Wall Street's criticism as nothing more than "wooden-headed stupidity" and smiled when his anti-trust policy was vindicated by the midterm election of 1902, which kept Republicans in control of Congress.[17] The election was a national referendum on his leadership. After his victory, with the popular wind at his back, he pushed legislation through Congress to prevent railroads from giving rebates and price reductions to favored shippers. This move was targeted at John D. Rockefeller's Standard Oil trust, which used its monopoly power to undercut the shipping costs of competitors.

Furious about Roosevelt's legislative attack on Standard Oil, Rockefeller sent telegrams to six Republican senators demanding the legislation—the Elkins Act—be stopped in Congress before it became law. He was particularly eager to prevent a provision of the legislation that forced trusts to open their books to government inspectors. After learning of the telegrams, Roosevelt pounced on the opportunity to expose Rockefeller's issuing orders to senators and promptly leaked the story to the newspapers. As he expected, the public erupted in indignation to learn its representatives were influenced, if not controlled, by the country's biggest trust magnate. The Elkins Act, along with its critical transparency amendment, passed through Congress with ease.

The Elkins Act had little impact on the Standard Oil monopoly, but represented a huge victory for Roosevelt. By taking on J. P. Morgan, he became the champion of the American people. Pitting himself against John D. Rockefeller—Morgan's equal in plutocratic infamy—he reinforced his standing with the public as a populist engaged in a triumphant war against "the money power." To achieve this objective, he had released information that suggested six Republican senators, members of his own party, were puppets on Rockefeller's string, which highlighted that Roosevelt was no machine politician who put party loyalty before the people and conscience.

Bolstered by his victory over Rockefeller, Roosevelt's popularity continued to grow throughout 1903. It was pushed higher the following year when the Supreme Court ruled, by a narrow five-to-four margin, that J. P. Morgan's Northern Securities railroad combination was in fact an illegal "restraint of trade" under the Sherman anti-trust law and must therefore be dissolved. The decision sealed for all time Roosevelt's reputation as a Trust Buster; he never achieved a greater victory in the realm of anti-trust policy. Editorializing on the ruling, the *New York World*, usually a fierce Roosevelt critic, praised his dramatic win over J. P. Morgan:

> Politically, the effect of the decision can hardly be exaggerated. It will greatly strengthen President Roosevelt as a candidate. People will love him for the enemies he has made. Mr. Cleveland lost popularity among the Democratic masses by not enforcing this law. Roosevelt will gain by enforcing it. It cannot now be said that the Republican Party is owned by the trusts.[18]

With the scalps of Morgan and Rockefeller hanging on his belt, the Trust Buster cruised to an easy victory in the 1904 presidential election. The public saw him as the implacable enemy of the plutocracy, as the champion of the American people against the "malefactors of great wealth." And yet, both Morgan and Rockefeller made large campaign contributions to his presidential campaign. Incredibly, twelve of the fifteen directors on the board of Northern Securities Company backed him for the White House that year, too, despite the fact that he had dissolved their combination.[19]

Morgan and Rockefeller's support for Roosevelt in 1904 was obviously driven by self-interest; they wished to maintain some influence with the administration even if they could not elect another safe man like Cleveland or McKinley. Nonetheless, their actions suggest they viewed Roosevelt as a political leader with redeeming conservative credentials in contrast to William Jennings Bryan, a radical they shunned as anathema. Although Roosevelt had broken the Northern Securities trust, Bryan wanted the federal government to seize control of the nation's railroads and thereby strike a blow against private property unmatched in American history. Roosevelt vehemently opposed the extreme policy of outright confiscation, a position that made him a sensible moderate in comparison.

The Elkins Act of 1903 put up obstacles to prevent railroads from lowering prices in the form of rebates to favored shippers. Roosevelt went one step further in 1906, persuading Congress to pass the Hepburn Act, which allowed the Interstate Commerce Commission to set the rates that railroads could charge shippers. While the Elkins and Hepburn laws were important legislative achievements—reinforcing the perception that Roosevelt was the enemy of Big Business—they did little to curb the growth of the trusts. The Hepburn law was more controversial. It gave government power to impose price controls for the first time but with restraints; the Interstate Commerce Commission could only set prices when shipping rates were challenged and proven to be artificial restraints on trade. Nor were the commission's decisions final, as the railroads were given thirty days to appeal rulings in federal court. Far from being an attack on capitalism, as libertarians sometimes charge, the Hepburn law was a check on the power of a monopolistic corporation (Standard Oil).

A BALANCED APPROACH

Roosevelt's crowning success in dissolving the Northern Securities combination hid his failure to dissolve any other large trust. While he did bring suit against Standard Oil, which led to its eventual dissolution after he left the White House, his enthusiasm for prosecuting trusts was nothing like that of his successor, William Howard Taft, as shown in this table:

Prosecutions for Violations of Sherman Anti-Trust Law			
President	Years Able to Enforce Law	Number of Prosecutions	Number per Year
Benjamin Harrison	2.0	7	3.5
Grover Cleveland	4.0	8	2.0
William McKinley	4.5	3	0.7
Theodore Roosevelt	**7.5**	**44**	**5.9**
William H. Taft	4.0	88	22.8
Woodrow Wilson	8.0	86	10.8
Warren Harding	2.5	49	19.6

Source: *The Washington Post*, October 29, 1935.

Nevertheless, Roosevelt did the American people an important service when he reversed the "look the other way" policy of his predecessors in the White House and enforced the Sherman anti-trust law in earnest for the first time. Yet he continues to be seen today by critics as a progressive enemy of Big Business when his enthusiasm for anti-trust prosecutions was considerably less fierce than that of Warren Harding and William Howard Taft, two of the most conservative presidents of the twentieth century. Libertarians who continue to carp about his administration need to be reminded of his relatively moderate anti-trust record and his favored approach of regulating corporations rather than breaking them apart, as well as his refusal to prosecute the U.S. Steel Company (also known as the Steel Trust).

The first corporation in American history to reach a market capitalization of $1 billion and the brainchild of J. P. Morgan, U.S. Steel was seemingly an ideal target for Roosevelt. The Justice Department had begun to investigate the company during his second term in the White House; a prosecution might have ensued but for the Panic of 1907, which threatened to throw the country into an economic depression. After one major New York bank failed and others seemed certain to follow, he gave the green light not to break but to enlarge U.S. Steel. Its leaders had asked him at an emergency White House meeting if they could buy the Tennessee Coal and Iron Company without interference from the Justice Department. The sale would infuse millions of dollars into a bank, on the brink of collapse, which held the Tennessee Coal and Iron Company's securities.

Subsequently, Roosevelt was attacked by his opponents for hypocrisy in denouncing "malefactors of great wealth" throughout his presidency, and then turning around and permitting the biggest trust in the country to expand its monopolistic power by acquiring its largest competitor. It was fair criticism, and highlights the difference between the image and substance of his anti-trust policy. The *New York Times*, for example, criticized TR's decision to approve U.S. Steel's purchase of the Tennessee Coal and Iron Company:

> U.S. Steel's request for his opinion was improper and ought never to have been made. There was much greater impropriety in his reply. His best answer would have been no answer at all. If he had to say something, the most he could with propriety say was to tell them to go ahead and take their own chances under advice of their own counsel. If he found that they had violated the law, they would hear from him. What he did tell them was that, while he had no advice to give, he felt it no public duty of his "to interpose any objection." If that meant anything it was, in effect, a dispensation from the obligation and the penalties of the law. It was a matter upon which Mr. Roosevelt had no call or any competence to say anything whatever. He is not a lawyer, he is not the law officer of the government, he is not a court. An opinion upon the legality of the proposed transaction would come properly only from the Attorney General, and he, of course, could not say in advance that the proposed purchase was in conformity with law.[20]

Sensitive to the criticism he received, TR put out his version of the merger to one of his newspaper allies, who quoted him as saying to the executives of U.S. Steel, who asked if he would approve the deal:

Gentlemen, in telling you that there seems to be no law to prevent your purchase of the Tennessee Steel company, I know I am assuming great responsibility. I might easily dodge it and tell you to consult your lawyers, but I know there is a great crisis at present, and this is not the time to shirk, because the business of the whole country is at stake. I take this action with my eyes open. Everybody will approve of it now because we all realize what a crisis it is. In a few months or in a year or so, if all goes well, and prosperity and confidence are restored, people will forget how terrible things look today, and then they will haul me over the coals as the protector of a great trust and as failing to prevent the gobbling up of one property by the owner of another. I know this is coming.[21]

The American people saw Roosevelt as devoted to their interests, but he was also intent on making the United States stronger; that meant ensuring the country's industry remained healthy and vibrant. His balanced approach of regulating the trusts without damaging the American economy was a wise policy. It was easy to condemn him for inconsistency in beginning his presidency by dissolving J. P. Morgan's Northern Securities railroad trust and ending it by helping Morgan's even bigger U.S. Steel trust expand its control over the industry. Yet in both cases, he acted in what he believed to be the country's best interests. In the first case, he helped protect the capitalist system by taking the energy out of the socialist movement. In the second, he helped prevent an economic depression by taking action to relieve the financial distress caused by the Panic of 1907. For these reasons, both of his most controversial trust-related actions deserve to be praised by posterity, not condemned.

CHAPTER EIGHT

SIDESTEPPING THE TARIFF THIRD RAIL

~

Theodore Roosevelt's moderate policy toward the trusts underlines the often neglected fact that he was a pro-business president, who saw economic growth, driven by business not the state, as central to American power.

It is also well to remember that by inheritance, Roosevelt was a free trader, but as president he made no attempt to lower the protective tariff wall that insulated the country's businesses from foreign competition. Support for the tariff was regarded as a pro-business (and conservative) policy, and Roosevelt left the tariff alone as a matter of economic and political prudence.

To see why one of the most reform-minded presidents refused to tackle what was arguably the greatest public-policy challenge of his generation, we must remember the unrelenting political strife that the tariff had produced from the time it became an integral part of the country's economy during George Washington's administration.

In our own time, the federal government relies primarily on the income tax to generate revenue. Throughout the nineteenth century, money flowed into the U.S. Treasury from duties imposed on manufactured goods and raw materials entering the country from foreign nations; proceeds from the sale of public lands; and excise taxes on spirits, tobacco, and other consumables. When this revenue system was first implemented in the 1790s, it enjoyed, for the most part, support across the political spectrum as a necessary means to pay off the young republic's large debt amassed during the Revolutionary War. The tax on spirits triggered an abortive uprising among backwoods distillers in Western Pennsylvania (the Whiskey Rebellion), but the rest of the revenue system met little or no opposition.

Acceptance of the tariff, however, ended in the South during the 1820s when Southern slaveholders running large plantations protested that protective tariffs boosted northern industry at the expense of southern agriculture. Free trade would have allowed the South to export products like cotton and tobacco and import competitively priced manufactured goods. Instead, Southern consumers bought manufactured goods that came with heavy import tariffs attached or that came from the North at prices higher than they would have been under a free trade regime. In addition, Southern exports were often hit with retaliatory tariffs, which limited the markets for Southern products and made them less profitable. Northern manufacturers, on the other hand, supported the tariff for blocking foreign competition and raising their profits, and workers in protected industries believed it provided them with jobs they might not otherwise have had and with wages that might otherwise be lower.

In the early 1830s, southern anger over the protective tariff grew so intense that South Carolina threatened to secede from the Union over the issue. Thirty years later, Southern hatred for the tariff was a leading cause of the Civil War. Even after Northern victory and Reconstruction ended such strident opposition to the tariff, agricultural areas of the country (the South and the West) favored a "revenue only" tariff, while the industrial Northeast and Midwest favored a "protective" tariff.

By the first decade of the twentieth century, the Northern view had won out. According to the *London Times*, reporting in 1909, "the American wage earner had become...imbued with the idea that the tariff keeps up his wages and increases the field of his employment." The newspaper also noted the magnetic attraction of jobs in industries that were protected, describing how "millions of laborers from all European countries, both protectionist and free trade, have migrated to this land of high protection and greatly improved their lot."[1]

The Republican Party, which dominated the federal government from 1861 to 1913, used its power to raise import duties to high levels. This policy accelerated the country's industrial growth, but also made the party appear an ally of Robber Baron industrialists. The Republican Party, the party of Abraham Lincoln, a party formed to oppose slavery (in the South) and polygamy (among Mormons), and support national development that offered greater opportunity for all—through homestead acts for settlers and support for railroads and schools and businesses (including its policy of high tariffs to protect "infant industries" and promote American companies that could supply, for domestic consumption, "blocked" imported items) had, to its critics, become the party of the rich and their interests rather than the interests of the people at large.

Theodore Roosevelt was a staunch Republican when he graduated from Harvard in 1880, but he was also a believer in free trade. He told a friend in the early 1880s, "as regards the tariff I am, as was my father...before me, a bit of a heretic when looked at with Republican eyes."[2] He joined the Cobden Club, an association of free traders with connections to Britain that advocated "the gradual and progressive modification of all our import duties in the direction of a simple tariff for revenue only."[3]

After he attended the Republican convention in Chicago in 1884, however, he had an abrupt change of heart. He was convinced he could not advance within the party without supporting its protection policy. Choosing expediency, he resigned his membership in the Cobden Club, and in 1886 publicly renounced his anti-protection heresy, telling a reporter during his mayoral campaign in simple but adamant fashion, "I am not a free trader."[4] He did not elaborate on his reasons, but it was clear: he had reversed his position.

Just as Roosevelt joined the conservatives in the Republican Party favoring a protective tariff, a movement of economic liberals, in both parties, was making it a matter of principle to oppose it. After his 1884 election victory, Democrat President Grover Cleveland made tariff reform the centerpiece of his domestic agenda, to the applause of most within his party. His effort to end protection, however, ended in political disaster, when he split his party over the issue and failed to gain the tariff reform he wanted. In 1888, though Cleveland won the popular vote, he lost the presidential election to the Republican Benjamin Harrison.

REPUBLICANS OVERPLAY THEIR HAND

Wrongly interpreting Cleveland's defeat as a mandate for protection, a wishful-thinking Republican Party made its own catastrophic political error two years later by passing the Tariff Act of 1890, which raised the average duty on imported goods and raw materials to nearly 50 percent.

Popularly known as the McKinley Tariff, the act was the high-water mark of protection, with the average import duty more than double the 20-percent level that Henry Clay found agreeable sixty years earlier. The move proved to be one of the greatest political blunders in American history as the Democrats won the House of Representatives by an enormous 141-seat margin over the Republicans in 1890. Two years later, President Harrison was thrown out of office largely because he signed the McKinley Tariff into law.

Observing the dramatic reversal of political fortunes produced by the tug of war between free traders and protectionists from 1884 to 1892, Roosevelt realized the tariff issue was a political third rail that was lethal to touch. Having forsaken his youthful dalliance with free trade, he was now in the protectionist camp but his support for the high tariff never rose above the level needed to pass his party's litmus test. He favored moderation, letting sleeping dogs lie, and was angered that his party had foolishly raised import duties to stratospheric levels in 1890. He was clearly frightened by the huge challenge of ending protection. Revising the tariff would have been a relatively easy task if the United States levied a single, flat-import duty across the board on all foreign manufactured goods and raw materials brought into the country. Instead of this simple system, the duty varied depending on the competitive threat each foreign import posed to American business.

Given the importance of the domestic steel industry, the McKinley Tariff imposed a heavy 75 percent duty on imported iron ore, artificially raising its price so high that it was unable to be sold at a profit in the American market. On the other hand, an esoteric raw material like uranium oxide, which was not produced in significant amounts in the United States (and which had no lobbying clout within Congress demanding its importation be blocked), was put on the so-called "free list," which allowed it to enter the country without any import duty. In between these two extremes was a range of import-duty levels across hundreds of different manufactured-product and raw-material categories, which were grouped into fourteen complicated tariff schedules. The confusing jumble of import-duty rates is similar in kind to today's income-tax code, with its dense maze of deductions, credits, and loopholes, impossible for anyone except an expert to understand. And just as businesses in our own time exert political pressure on Congress to amend the tax code in their favor, businesses then employed lobbyists to keep import duties as high as possible to protect their commercial interests from foreign competition.

TR SIDESTEPS THE CONTROVERSY

In refusing to touch the tariff during his presidency, Roosevelt hoped to avoid repeating the mistake both political parties had made by entangling themselves in a controversial issue, one that he found daunting; economics was not his favorite subject. "I get very much puzzled at times on questions of finance and the tariff,"[5] he admitted.

In addition, Roosevelt did not see tariff reform as a national imperative. TR wrote to Henry Cabot Lodge in 1909, "What we have to meet is not an actual need, but a mental condition among our people, who believe there ought to be a change." When Lodge showed his letter to Nelson Aldrich, the high priest of protection in the Republican Party responded with glee: "He put the whole situation in those few lines. He is the greatest politician we have ever had. We are dealing with a mental condition and that is the exact trouble with the situation."[6] (More than a century later, we can see that TR, Aldrich, and the rest of the party's old guard were out of touch. The country needed tariff reform to relieve not only the financial burden imposed on the entire population via higher prices but also the heavy drag that limited competition placed on the nation's economy. The Smoot-Hawley tariff passed in 1930, which smothered foreign trade when the country needed it most, showed these negative consequences clearly during the Great Depression.)

Roosevelt also had other things on his mind, particularly the struggle for power between the world's great powers. Compared to this contest, determining import duties on opera glasses or iron ore seemed trivial and mundane. He gladly left the complexities of the tariff to cold-blooded souls like McKinley who were adept with numbers, and brave but foolish reformers like Cleveland, who were overconfident in their ability to slay a fierce political dragon. When dealing with the tariff, he followed the dictum of Shakespeare's Sir John Falstaff, who famously declared: "Discretion is the better part of valor."

A lack of interest in finance and economics and a determination to avoid political danger kept Roosevelt far away from the tariff third rail during the decade that preceded his entrance into the White House. And a historic ruling in 1895 gave him a further shove in that direction when the Supreme Court declared the income tax unconstitutional.

The reactionary decision came in response to the Democrats' tariff-reform law of 1894, the Wilson-Gorman Tariff Act, which imposed an income tax on wealthy Americans to replace the revenue lost when import duties were lowered. President Cleveland, who earnestly wanted tariff reform, was appalled at the way members of his own party had amended the bill in favor of protectionism to appease special interests. He let the act become law, as only a modest improvement to existing law, without signing it or supporting it. His free-trade Democrat allies were further disheartened when the Supreme Court struck down a key component of the law, ruling by a five-to-four margin that the income tax was unconstitutional because it was not apportioned equally among the states. With the income tax now off the table, tariff reform became practically impossible because lower import duties inevitably produced large budget deficits. Among that frugal generation, deficit spending had little support.

But tariff reform still did. It was one popular cause Roosevelt, as president, declined to embrace, telling a friend: "I do not wish to split my own party wide open on the tariff question unless some good is to come."[7] When challenged by the press to explain his tariff policy, he responded that he wanted Congress to create a special bipartisan tariff commission empowered to lower or raise import duties on specific manufactured goods and raw materials as needed to promote the best interests of the country. This sounded like a sensible idea, but really was an empty proposal; he knew Congress would never voluntarily transfer one of its key powers—control over the country's revenue generating engine—to an unelected body (imagine Congress today giving its power to lower or raise income taxes to another body). His proposal was a non-starter but good politics.

TARIFFS AND TRUSTS: TWO SIDES OF THE SAME COIN

Roosevelt's insincerity in floating his tariff commission proposal was matched by his insincerity in contending—both during and after his presidency—that because the protective tariff was "not any appreciable factor in maintaining our so-called trusts,"[8] his trust-busting did not need to lower import duties to be effective. This argument might be explained by his limited knowledge of finance and economics but his understanding of the tariff issue was not poor. He must have known the Sherman anti-trust law was enacted to prevent the illegal "restraint of trade" and that the protective tariff was by definition a "restraint of trade," albeit one sanctioned by the government and thus entirely legal. Like all monopolistic enterprises, the trusts wanted to eliminate competition to corner markets and raise prices, and thereby increase profits. To achieve this end, they needed to eliminate competition that existed at home as well as that which came from abroad. They could achieve the former by bankrupting or absorbing their domestic competitors but foreign competitors could not be dispensed with as easily; they were safeguarded in their distant home markets. To eliminate the threat, the trusts needed the help of the federal government to erect a tariff wall that made the price of foreign imports so high that they could not be sold in the American market.

One did not need to be an economist to see that a monopoly could not exist in the United States if foreign competitors were allowed to trade without restraint in the American market. Even Theodore Havemeyer, the head of the notorious Sugar Trust (which imposed an indirect tax on every American family by raising food prices), admitted as much when he told a congressional committee, "the protective tariff was the father of the trust."[9] That the Sugar Trust, in particular, benefited immensely from the protective tariff can be seen in the fierce opposition it threw up when Roosevelt tried to lower the duty on sugar from Cuba and the Philippines, and in the way it blocked the annexation of Hawaii out of fear that cheap sugar from it would flood the American market. It lost a political slugfest to keep Cuban sugar out of the American market but succeeded in barring sugar from the Philippines; its lobbying clout evaporated when victory over Spain in 1898 became the government's overriding concern.

Roosevelt's attempt to keep the trusts and the tariff in two separate buckets made little sense from the standpoint of helping American consumers, who were hurt by trade restraints whether they came from monopolies crushing their domestic competitors or the U.S. government maintaining a trade wall to keep out foreign competitors. But it did make sense, to its apologists at least, because the tariff was presumed to create a great many jobs through its support of domestic businesses; and, of course, it maintained America's long-standing economic model, which, for the most part, seemed to be successful. Weighing just as heavily on Roosevelt as these arguments was the argument that the Republican Party could not afford an internal fight on tariff reform.

It is easy to criticize Theodore Roosevelt for inaction, but in hindsight he did the right thing. All wise leaders prioritize and focus on policies with a reasonable chance of success. For this reason, it was prudent to emphasize trust-busting at the expense of tariff reform. It was no accident that a Democratic president, Woodrow Wilson, and a Democrat-controlled Congress managed to end fifty long years of high protection, helped by the income tax authorized by the Sixteenth Amendment to the Constitution in 1913, which allowed Democrats to avoid an $80 billion budget deficit by taxing the earnings of wealthy Americans. President Roosevelt did not have the luxury of revenue from an income tax—nor the enthusiastic support of an anti-protection party the way Wilson did—to aid him had he attempted tariff reform.

CHAPTER NINE

NEGLECTING CURRENCY/ BANKING REFORM

~

D espite all the hullaballoo about trust-busting, in December 1901, the *London Times* noted that Theodore Roosevelt's domestic policy was driven first and foremost by a desire to maintain "economic stability."[1] Stability meant prosperity, prosperity made for a wealthier, stronger America, and not incidentally national prosperity improved Roosevelt's odds for reelection.

Roosevelt's often unnoticed cautious conservatism in economic matters can also be seen in his hands-off approach to currency and banking reform. He was an unwavering supporter of "sound money," that is to say, of the gold standard, which guaranteed that the money circulated was backed by gold rather than less valuable metals like silver or, as it is today, by the mere promise of the "full faith and credit" of the U.S. government. Like J. P. Morgan, he viewed it as the bedrock of the country's financial system and as an impenetrable fortress wall that protected amassed capital.

Despite pressure from leftist progressives, led by Democrat William Jennings Bryan, Roosevelt made no attempt during his presidency to reform the currency, which depended on the available supply of gold to maintain its value at a healthy level. Reformers protested that the gold-backed dollar was vulnerable to deflation, which could contract the economy and produce financial panics, if the global mining of gold failed to keep pace with economic expansion. The problem was worsened by the absence of a central bank, thanks to Andrew Jackson's reckless decision to dissolve the Bank of the United States in the 1830s. Critics argued that the country needed to update its antiquated financial system by making its currency more elastic and creating a new central bank to oversee the nation's monetary policy, which was largely controlled by private-citizen financiers not accountable to the American people.

That Roosevelt, the conservative reformer, failed to address the currency and banking issue is not surprising given his lack of interest in finance and economics. From his study of American history, he knew that the paper money issued by Congress during the Revolutionary War became virtually worthless ("not worth a Continental" was a popular saying in the 1780s), reinforcing his belief that sound money backed by gold was needed to prevent inflation. In this attitude, he was unmistakably the grandson of C. V. S. Roosevelt, the founder of Chemical Bank, who "never failed to meet his obligations in gold."

So Roosevelt not only embraced the gold standard, but also denounced William Jennings Bryan for his 1896 plan to dramatically increase the money supply by allowing the currency to be backed by silver in addition to gold at a sixteen-to-one ratio. Bryan was right in principle: the health of the American economy depends on a money supply sufficient to equal the amount of commercial activity taking place in the economy. Much of the sluggish economic growth of the 1890s could be traced to the deflationary effect caused by the global scarcity of gold, which became more plentiful when new mines were opened in Alaska and South Africa.

Roosevelt, of course, could not understand factors that are only seen in hindsight. The conventional wisdom was that inflation was an evil that had to be prevented at all costs, and that the only means to that end was firm adherence to the gold standard. When the gold supply became scarce in the mid-1890s and deflation set in, lowering the prices farmers could get for their crops, agricultural sections of the United States demanded a change in the monetary system. Fearful the abandonment of the gold standard would greatly decrease their wealth, the country's bankers and industrialists poured money into William McKinley's campaign to defeat the populist movement that threatened their fortunes.

This was in some ways ironic, because as a congressman McKinley had himself once been a "Silver Republican." He had supported the Sherman Silver Purchase Act of 1890, designed by his fellow Ohioan, Republican Senator John Sherman, chairman of the Senate Finance Committee. The modest—and, as it proved, unsuccessful and even counterproductive—reform, made special Treasury Coin Notes redeemable in either silver or gold (investors unfortunately preferred the latter). It was repealed as a financial necessity in 1893, at the request of President Grover Cleveland, during that year's financial panic.

It was equally ironic—given the myths that have grown up about his progressivism—that the great reformer Theodore Roosevelt stood with America's wealthiest business interests athwart the pitchfork revolution Bryan led to throw out the gold standard.

NEGLECTING THE HAMILTONIAN TRADITION

The American economy had benefited immensely from the Bank of the United States created by Alexander Hamilton during the early 1790s. Hamilton's bank helped restore the credit of the United States at a time when the young republic was heavily in debt and increased the availability of credit to the business community, thereby spurring economic growth. Roosevelt should have logically been a strong advocate for creating a central bank controlled by Washington rather than Wall Street so that the country would not have to humble itself before an unelected plutocrat like J. P. Morgan. Roosevelt admired Hamilton but his study of Andrew Jackson's war on the Bank of the United States convinced him that the country's first central bank had "too much power for its own or outsiders' good." He sympathized with Jackson's policy, remarking that Old Hickory "had much justice on his side" and that "the destruction of the bank was by no means altogether to be regretted."[2]

Roosevelt's indifference toward currency and banking reform was understandable in light of the country's prosperity during his presidency and the silence of public opinion on the matter. But the Panic of 1907 shook the nation's financial system and made it plain that the United States needed a modern banking system to allow private banks to keep their doors open during "runs."

TR had ample time to push Congress to enact legislation after the 1907 crisis. At that moment, he might have joined the chorus of financial experts and called for the creation of a central bank to provide financial relief to stressed banks during future panics. But he did not, instead allowing his successor Woodrow Wilson to sign into law the creation of the Federal Reserve banking system in 1913. Why didn't Roosevelt push for a central bank when he had the opportunity? Political considerations were likely the prime factor. In a letter to a trusted friend, he admitted in November 1907, "our fiscal system is not good from the purely fiscal side" and that a central bank would be "a very good thing" for the country. But he believed a bank would likely excite public anger as it had in the 1830s and as a result might trigger social unrest:

> Certainly, I believe that at least a central bank, with branch banks, in each of the states (I mean national banks, of course) would be good, but I doubt whether our people would support either scheme at present.... There is this grave objection.... Sooner or later there would be in that bank some insolent man whose head would be turned by his own power and ability, who would fail to realize other types of ability and the limitations upon his power, and would by his actions awaken the slumbering popular distrust and cause a storm in which he would be as helpless as a child, and which would

overwhelm not only him but other men and other things of far more importance.[3]

Roosevelt's description of "some insolent man" at the head of a new central bank who would "cause a storm" was a reference to Nicholas Biddle, the head of the Bank of the United States, who President Andrew Jackson vilified. Nevertheless, Roosevelt's inaction in dealing with the country's currency and banking challenges might very well have exacerbated the animosity he felt for Wilson, who took the opportunity, which Roosevelt had forfeited, to give the United States a financial system as strong as that of Great Britain.

Roosevelt should have known that the Bank of England was one of the main pillars of Britain's power along with its vast colonial empire, the Suez Canal, and her impressive navy. He wanted the United States to have its own colonial empire (anchored by the Philippines), its own strategic canal (in Panama), and its own gigantic navy (he doubled its size) but at the same time opposed creating a central bank. This was a major oversight for a man who devoted his whole life to increasing the geopolitical power of the United States by following what was, essentially, the template Britain had used to become the world's greatest power during the nineteenth century.

It seems clear that Roosevelt did not fully appreciate the importance of financial power as a driver of national power, even though, as an accomplished historian, he should have known that Britain's victory in its long war against Napoleon's France a century earlier had been won as much by the Bank of England as by the Royal Navy.

When it came to advancing American interests, Roosevelt did not believe that the Federal Reserve banking system was quite as important as colonial territories, the Panama Canal, and the Great White Fleet. In part, this was because he was more of a military and naval historian than an economist, in part it was because of the lessons he took from American political history, and in part it was because he was, at bottom, a nationalist who did not want an entity, like the Federal Reserve, outside control of the government, driving the economy.

CHAPTER TEN

SETTING THE
MODEL FOR
LABOR DISPUTES

~

W ith his announcement in February 1902 that he intended to dissolve the Northern Securities railroad combination of J. P. Morgan, Theodore Roosevelt meant to transform the Republican Party of "Big Business" into the party of "the people." As he phrased it, he ended the "old commercial conservatism" that reached its peak with McKinley's election in 1896 and replaced it with "the Lincoln Republicanism of the party's first decade."[1] The political impact of his trust-busting was enhanced by another equally dramatic action he took early in his presidency when he intervened in the Anthracite Coal Strike.

At the beginning of the twentieth century, coal was the principal fuel used to heat homes, schools, and businesses; as such it was an essential commodity during the winter months in the northern United States. When miners of anthracite coal in eastern Pennsylvania decided in the spring of 1902 to strike to secure higher wages and force the mine operators to recognize their union, the United Mine Workers of America, there was no immediate crisis since temperatures were warm—a fact that helped keep public opinion from swinging against the striking miners. If the labor dispute was not settled by the time cold weather set in, the mood of the country would undoubtedly change.

Monitoring the coal strike from Washington, President Roosevelt at first saw no need to involve himself in the controversy. The Constitution gave him no explicit power to interfere in a labor dispute, so in June 1902 he rejected the plea of the New York Board of Trade when it asked him to mediate a settlement between the 147,000 striking coal miners and the small group of mine operators. Similar pleas were sent to J. P. Morgan, who had helped arbitrate a resolution to a coal miners' strike in 1900; but this time Morgan also refused to intervene.

Roosevelt did, however, ask Carroll D. Wright, his Commissioner of Labor, to report to him on the strike. Pressure continued on TR to intervene, including a petition from the people of Wilkes-Barre, Pennsylvania in late August, which read, in part:

> Since the inception of the barbarous and senseless struggle in the anthracite coal region, we, the non-combatants, who stand upon neutral ground, have suffered.... We had hoped for much upon J. P. Morgan's return.... Mr. Morgan has met with his henchmen, and the edict has gone forth: "There will be no settlement, no arbitration, no conciliation, no mediation, no concessions. The fight must go on." ...Is J. Pierpont Morgan greater than the people? Is he mightier than the government? Will he be permitted to retain his menacing power? It is time the people should speak. It is time that their voices should be heard.[2]

With the strike continuing as autumn began, Roosevelt realized he needed to involve himself to avert an economic catastrophe. Intervention would also emphasize his reformist, trust-buster image and contrast him again with J. P. Morgan, who was a major employer of coal miners and was assumed to be on the side of the mine operators. In October 1902

Roosevelt asked the head of the United Mine Workers union, John Mitchell, and the mine operators to come to the White House for a conference to discuss the matter "in regard to the failure of the coal supply, which has become a matter of vital concern to the whole nation."[3] The simple invitation was a precedent-setting move. No American president had up to that point attempted to mediate a labor dispute.

STRONG-ARMING THE MINE OPERATORS

His decision to intervene cheered the striking miners, whose negotiating position was weakening as winter approached. The mine operators, waiting patiently for victory to fall into their lap, were angered by the president's summons, viewing it as a lifeline to the striking miners. Unable to reject the invitation, out of fear the public would view it as rude intransigence, they resolved to maintain an inflexible front, putting out word to the newspapers that the conference would "show the miners that no third party, not even the President of the United States, can budge the operators from their position, and that once this is realized the strikers will weaken."[4]

As good as their word, the mine operators refused to give an inch in the discussions at the White House that followed. Brushing aside their opposition, Roosevelt promptly created a board of inquiry to investigate the strike and make recommendations about how a fair settlement could be reached. Roosevelt persuaded, in principle, former President Grover Cleveland to join the Anthracite Coal Strike Commission he had created. Cleveland was reluctant, because he thought the miners should return to work while negotiations continued, and in the end Roosevelt removed him from the commission as both sides in the dispute rejected Cleveland as an arbitrator.

Next, and more important, the president ordered a detachment of the U.S. Army under Major General Schofield to stand ready to seize the coal mines and operate them if needed. Once these preparations were made, he gave the mine operators an ultimatum: agree to abide by the findings of the presidential commission or watch the U.S. Army take control of their property.

Faced with this outcome, the mine operators backed down and the coal strike ended. J. P. Morgan, as it turned out, played a role, after Elihu Root (TR's secretary of war), asked him to help the administration negotiate a compromise, which he did.

It was Roosevelt, however, not Morgan, who was the hero of the hour when the strike ended on October 23, 1902, and his triumph appeared to boost his trust-busting efforts. As the *London Times* editorialized:

> In the most quiet and unobtrusive manner President Roosevelt has done a very big thing and an entirely new thing.... His personal reputation and prestige are enormously enhanced.... Our New York correspondent tells us that this strike, or rather the incidents of its termination, have brought home to the American people with greater clearness than ever the national dangers of gigantic trusts.[5]

Although Roosevelt's popularity soared, the American people were not informed about the most controversial aspect of the strike's resolution, his presidential threat to use the U.S. Army to seize and operate the mines. Future presidents went beyond threatening to use military force to override private-property rights in the alleged national interest. Woodrow Wilson was the first, ordering ten thousand soldiers to the Pacific Northwest in 1917 to operate lumber facilities to ensure an ample supply of spruce wood needed to construct military aircraft during World War I. Thirty years later, Harry Truman used a variation of TR's gambit and was about to ask Congress to draft striking railroad workers into the U.S. Army when his threat persuaded them to return to work.

While some might decry Roosevelt's strong-arm tactics, his conduct was more restrained than that of his predecessor, Grover Cleveland, who deployed the U.S. Army to break the Pullman Strike in Chicago in 1894. Cleveland famously declared, "If it takes the entire Army and Navy to deliver a postcard in Chicago that card will be delivered."[6] His use of the military to settle a domestic dispute has been condemned by historians as an action inspired by his pro-business attorney general, Richard Olney, who wanted to crush the strike to create an object lesson that would help suppress future labor uprisings.

By allowing the U.S. Army to be used as the tool of railroad magnates, by refusing to help broker a peaceful settlement, and by ignoring Illinois Governor John Peter Altgeld, a Democrat, who thought he could handle his state's affairs (Illinois was the focal point of the national strike), Cleveland made mistakes that Roosevelt did not. Roosevelt assembled a commission representing all points of view, worked with Pennsylvania's governor to help the state manage the crisis, and personally helped mediate an end to the strike. His big stick industrial diplomacy was successful and he never had to act on his threat to deploy the U.S. Army in the coal fields.

Unlike Grover Cleveland, Calvin Coolidge (who broke the Boston Police Strike when he was governor of Massachusetts, famously saying: "There is no right to strike against the public safety"), and Ronald Reagan (who fired the nation's striking air-traffic controllers), Roosevelt sided, for the most part, with labor in the coal miners' strike, if for no other reason than that the miners' representatives seemed less intransigent than the mine operators. The United Mine Workers were willing to end the dispute via arbitration by a neutral presidential commission (which gave mine workers the modest 10 percent wage increase the union desired).

TR, however, was no knee-jerk supporter of the labor movement. For instance, he ensured that government workers were employed under "open-shop" rules so that they could not be compelled to join a union against their will. For TR, the common thread was always acting, as president, in what he saw as the national interest.

CHAPTER ELEVEN

PROTECTING CONSUMER HEALTH AND SAFETY

~

H enry Ford is often given credit for building up the American economy at the beginning of the twentieth century. Ford startled the country with the announcement that he would pay the workers in his automobile plants the unheard-of manufacturing labor wage of five dollars a day. This was a landmark moment: it gave Ford's workers disposable income that they could use to spend on consumer goods like the company's Model T automobile, creating an example that other industries would eventually adopt. Rising household incomes increased demand for manufactured goods, giving entrepreneurs greater incentive to start new businesses, tapping into a rapidly expanding pool of consumers who had more money to spend. In this way, the economy began to shift from large industrial concerns like U.S. Steel to consumer manufacturers like Procter and Gamble; and advertising for consumer dollars became a major business as well.

Roosevelt's enthusiastic embrace of technological innovations involving weapons of war—he was the first president to fly in an airplane and the first to travel underwater in a submarine—has created the impression he was focused on the future. But he longed for the simpler life he had enjoyed throughout his youth, preferring horses to automobiles and a mode of living that was fading fast during his presidency. That devotion was revealed by an anecdote told by the Japanese diplomat Kentaro Kaneko, who stayed at his Sagamore Hill home in 1904. Kaneko found it thrilling to be in "the home of the head of a great nation," but was astonished to see the house of such an exalted leader still "lighted with kerosene lamps" while he, Kaneko, had been using electric light at his home in Japan for fifteen years.

Failing to see the emergence of the consumer economy, Roosevelt could not have realized that it meant the death knell of the protective tariff, as increased consumer purchasing power made voters increasingly sensitive to higher prices. This phenomenon had occurred in Britain sixty years earlier and, as a consequence, had compelled the British government to dismantle its protective tariff and replace it with an income tax. President Wilson later travelled down a path that Roosevelt feared to tread, but in TR's defense, Wilson did not risk political suicide by implementing his pro-consumer policy of tariff reduction. His party was fully behind the reform. Unable to do anything about the tariff, Roosevelt protected consumers in a different way by enacting new regulations that ensured they were informed about the ingredients contained in food products and that the food they purchased was safe to eat.

IMPROVING THE SAFETY OF FOOD AND DRUGS

In our own time, the news occasionally reports that someone has died of food tainted with E. coli, salmonella, or other bacteria. Such tragedies are rare; food manufacturers must adhere to rules imposed on them by the Food and Drug Administration (FDA), a federal agency that compels them to meet reasonable safety standards. When Americans bite into a McDonald's hamburger or swallow a capsule of Tylenol, they do not put their life at risk. And they owe Theodore Roosevelt a debt of gratitude, since he was the de facto "father of the FDA" by enacting the first laws to improve the safety of food and drugs.

The first of these was the Pure Food and Drug Act, which was enacted in early 1906 after fifteen years of fierce resistance from "the representatives of the great drug houses, of the manufacturers of prepared foods, of distilleries, and of the proprietors of supposedly secret patent medicines, which bombarded Congress with assertions that their lives, their liberty and their property were all at stake" if desperately needed safety-related reforms were implemented.[1] He defeated this powerful lobby, compelling food and drug manufacturers to place labels on their products that accurately listed their ingredients.

On the same day he signed the Pure Food law, Roosevelt also approved the Federal Meat Inspection Act. This second consumer-protection law was the outcome of a national drama involving the acclaimed muckraker, Upton Sinclair, whose novel *The Jungle* shocked the country by revealing the manner in which Chicago meat packers produced the food they sold to consumers. Roosevelt responded to the book's allegations and pressured Congress—against the wishes of the meat packing industry—into creating tough legislation to fix the problem.

A cattle rancher before he reached the White House, Roosevelt sympathized on a personal level with the nation's meat industry, understanding its workings as few people did. But as president of the United States, his duty was to protect the interests of the American people as a whole. One newspaper account of alleged abuses at Chicago meat-packing plants described:

- Carcasses of hogs which had died of cholera made into lard and grease for use in making sardine oil
- Hams in a putrefied condition injected with chemicals, while other chemicals were used to dye bad meat
- Cattle which died from disease used to make tinned beef
- Mutton which was really goats' flesh
- Sausages manufactured from scrapings of floors liberally treated with embalming chemicals

- Meat workers being caught in machinery and mutilated, without stopping the machinery, so that human flesh was mixed in with the canned food and sausages[2]

Questions remained as to whether Sinclair's disturbing allegations were true, so President Roosevelt took the reasonable step of sending an investigator, Charles Neill, to look into the meat packing plants in Chicago. When Neill returned to Washington in June 1906, his report-in-hand largely confirmed Sinclair's exposé, prompting the president to tell Congress he wanted a law that would provide "a drastic and thoroughgoing inspection by the federal government of all stock yards and packing houses and of their products,"[3] adding he thought "the expense of the inspection should be paid by a fee levied on each animal slaughtered" to ensure the inspection regime would be fully funded.[4]

Fearing profits would suffer as a result of this regulatory effort, the meat packers rose up in protest. They used their influence with Congress to water down the legislation and succeeded to such an extent that Roosevelt erupted in fury when he read the first draft of the meat-inspection bill. Prior to this, he had negotiated a gentleman's agreement with the meat packers, telling them he would keep Neill's report secret if they acquiesced to his plan. He kept his word; the meat packers did not. So he released Neill's report to the American people, using public opinion to persuade Congress to do the right thing, just as he had when he leaked the news that John D. Rockefeller had sent telegrams to six U.S. senators ordering them to stop the Elkins anti-trust legislation in 1903.

Once again, his populist strategy triumphed as the country denounced the meat packers as fiends after reading the Neill report. Congressional opposition collapsed under the weight of public anger, and TR obtained most of the legislation he wanted, agreeing to drop his request that the meat packers pay for a new inspection system in lieu of an automatic annual appropriation of $3 million to cover the cost.

ROOSEVELT'S REGULATORY LEGACY

It is true that Theodore Roosevelt, through laws like the Federal Meat Inspection Act of 1906, made the federal government a much greater regulatory power than it had ever been before. As the *New York Times* noted at the time:

> During no session of Congress since the foundation of the government has so much been done, first, to extend the federal power of regulation and control over the business of the country, and, second, to cure and prevent abuses of corporation privilege.... It was President Roosevelt who, with a zeal and energy that often overstepped the traditional limits of the Executive function, urged upon Congress compliance with the people's will, and it is to him, as every qualified and impartial observer must admit, that the credit of the larger work of the session is chiefly due. Without him we are afraid there would have been no [Railroad] Rate bill, no Meat Inspection bill.... It is centralization—there is no doubt of that. But the impulses that brought it about arose from no personal ambition or dangerous spirit of usurpation at the capital. It originated in the desire and the will of the people themselves seeking protection against corporation greed and lawlessness.[5]

But in no way was the new regulatory regime intended to be an endless inflator of big government. As president, Roosevelt encouraged Congress to exercise such regulatory power as was necessary to break up monopolies and protect consumers from, essentially, fraudulently advertised or even dangerous products. Far from being an enemy of business, he protected free markets by ensuring that they operated in ways that built consumer trust, that encouraged competition, and that prevented consumer harm. Far from being an indictment of his conservatism, President Roosevelt's record in protecting consumer health and safety is proof of it. He was no libertarian ideologue to be sure. Instead, he was a conservative statesman who made prudent and pragmatic use of government power to protect the safety of the American people—and that is as worthy a conservative goal in domestic policy as it is in foreign policy.

CHAPTER TWELVE

CONSERVING NATURAL RESOURCES

~

W hen it came to politically charged issues like the trusts, Theodore Roosevelt pursued a moderate approach, occupying a position slightly ahead of the American people but not far from the safe anchor of favorable public opinion. His policy on conserving natural resources, however, attracted relatively little opposition and thus was pursued with maximum force. As a result, he achieved arguably the most visible achievement of his presidency by unleashing a conservation movement that remains a force today. As one astute commentator has pointed out, "millions of Americans see him each year in national parks or national forests which he created for them, and for their children, and for their children's children."[1]

Roosevelt's aggressive conservation policy included:

- The addition of 150 million acres of timberland to the nation's forest reserves (the three previous presidential

administrations combined had reserved roughly 50 million acres)[2]

- The creation of fifty-one bird refuges (he was the first
  president to establish a federal wildlife refuge)
- Signing into law the Antiquities Act of 1906, which gave
  the president the ability to protect areas with unique physical and cultural characteristics by proclaiming them
  "national monuments"
- Taking advantage of this new power, he created sixteen
  national monuments, including Devil's Tower in Wyoming, the Grand Canyon in Arizona, and Muir Woods in
  California
- Doubling the number of national parks from five to ten
  (including Crater Lake in Oregon and Mesa Verde in
  Colorado) to complement those established before he
  became president (Yellowstone, Yosemite, Sequoia, General Grant, and Mount Rainier)
- Holding an unprecedented national conference on conservation at the White House in 1908, attended by five
  hundred of the country's most influential leaders, including forty-four state governors and most members of Congress[3]

American history places the magnitude of Roosevelt's achievement
in context. With a huge continent to conquer, the early settlers cared
little for conservation (a word that only came into popular use because
Roosevelt regularly used it to describe his policy[4]), because the natural
resources around them seemed inexhaustible. Some thoughtful men in
the early days of the republic were taken with the natural beauty of the
country's magnificent landscape, like Thomas Jefferson, who declared
that the beauty of the Potomac River cutting through the Blue Ridge
Mountains was a scene "worth a voyage across the Atlantic."[5] But most
Americans did not have the luxury to indulge in the aesthetic delights of
nature. They were more concerned with making a living from nature.

Public attitudes began to change after the Civil War, when rapid industrial development and the concentration of the population in cities made wilderness areas more unique and valuable than before. Symbolizing this shift, the creation of Yellowstone National Park in 1872 marked the first major action by the federal government to protect land important to the entire nation. In the two decades that followed, however, many of the nation's forests were plundered by the lumber industry in their quest to meet the insatiable appetite of the United States for wood in the industrial age.

Estimating the extent of timber razed during this period is difficult, but the problem was big enough to spur action by Congress, which passed a Timber Culture law in the 1880s, which attempted to replenish the nation's dwindling timber supply by requiring those who acquired land from the federal government to plant new trees on one-quarter of their new property. As this step proved inadequate, efforts to solve the problem were followed-up in 1891 with far more substantial legislation—the Forest Reserve Act—which gave the president the power to "set apart and reserve in any state or territory having public lands bearing forests...as a public reservation."[6]

The Forest Reserve Act empowered the president to bypass political opposition in Congress (representing the powerful lumber lobby) and to save endangered forests from commercial exploitation. The historian Charles A. Beard called the act "one of the most noteworthy measures ever passed in the history of the nation."[7] This was high but merited praise.

President Benjamin Harrison signed the Forest Reserve Act into law at the insistence of his able secretary of the interior, John Noble, who subsequently persuaded him to reserve vast swaths of forest land in California (including the San Gabriel and San Bernardino mountains around Los Angeles, and the Sierra mountain range south of Yosemite National Park), Wyoming (1.2 million acres near Yellowstone National Park), and Washington State (the area around Mount Rainier). President Grover Cleveland reserved more than 21 million acres of vulnerable forestland during his second administration (1893–1897). Harrison and

Cleveland were outdoorsmen who loved to hunt and fish, and wanted future generations to be able to do likewise in an appealing natural environment. Roosevelt took their efforts and dramatically expanded them.

ROOSEVELT LAUNCHES THE CONSERVATION MOVEMENT

Having studied nature throughout his youth and nearly becoming a professional naturalist after college, Roosevelt took a keen interest in the subject of saving the nation's forests, and also in preserving the game they contained. As he told a fellow nature lover:

> I would like to see all harmless wild things, but especially all birds, protected in every way.... Spring would not be Spring without song birds.... The destruction of the Wild Pigeon and the Carolina Paroquet has meant a loss as severe as if the Catskills and the Palisades were taken away. When I hear of the destruction of a species, I feel as if all the works of some great writer had perished, as if we had lost all instead of only part of Polybius or Livy.[8]

As much as Roosevelt loved the natural world for its beauty, he also loved to hunt big game and was disturbed to see it rapidly depleting as civilization overwhelmed the North American wilderness. By the time he began to hunt in the West during the early 1880s, the buffalo were nearly extinct. By the end of the decade, other species began to dwindle to levels that made them difficult to find in the wild. A friend, George Bird Grinnell, the editor of *Forest and Stream* magazine, shared the same concerns. To combat this negative trend, the two men decided to form the Boone and Crockett Club with five objectives in mind:

1. To promote manly sport with the rifle;
2. To promote...exploration of the wild and unknown;

3. To work for the preservation of wild game;
4. To…record observations on the habits and natural history of the various wild animals;
5. To bring among the members interchange of opinions and ideas on hunting, travel and exploration.[9]

The role of the Boone and Crockett Club in igniting the conservation movement is confirmed by Grinnell, who said in 1913, "Perhaps no single thing that Roosevelt did for conservation had so far-reaching an effect as the establishment of the Boone and Crockett Club."[10] He was alluding to the success Roosevelt had in recruiting like-minded men of prominence into the club, many of whom were powerful political leaders in Washington, men who would eventually put their full weight behind the Forest Reserve Act of 1891 and support the conservation movement. As president of the Boone and Crockett Club during its first five years, Roosevelt the private citizen led the embryonic conservation effort, which was mostly limited to upper class outdoorsmen like himself. In 1899, however, he was elected governor of New York and, for the first time, was in a position to implement conservation policies. To achieve this end, he turned to his friend Gifford Pinchot, one of the few Americans at that time with an expertise in forestry, having studied the subject in Europe. Pinchot's conservation philosophy was based on the utilitarian idea that forests should be managed to become a sustainable resource for the nation, guaranteeing a steady supply of timber and related benefits to the population over time. Roosevelt found this practical approach consistent with his own ideas, which were expressed in his Second Annual Message as governor of New York in January 1900:

We need to have our system of forestry gradually developed and conducted along scientific principles. When this is done it will be possible to allow marketable timber to be cut everywhere without damage to the forests—indeed, with positive advantage to them. But until lumbering is thus conducted…we cannot afford to suffer it at all in the state forests. Unrestrained

greed means the ruin of the great woods and the drying up of
the sources of the rivers.[11]

CONSERVATION:
A NATION-BUILDING IMPERATIVE

Today, most Americans assume Roosevelt set aside millions of acres
of forest land during his presidency in order to create national parks that
Americans could visit during their summer vacations. While the recre-
ational angle is part of the story, TR's overriding objective was to protect
the natural wealth of the nation. He wanted to maintain a few special
forests (like those along the Pacific coast, which held ancient and therefore irreplaceable Sequoia trees) in pristine condition so that they could
be marveled at in perpetuity as objects of beauty. But the rest of his goal
was to "allow marketable timber to be cut everywhere without damage
to the forests." In his Arbor Day message of 1907, he repeated this theme,
declaring, "A true forest is not merely a storehouse of wood, but, as it
were, a factory of wood, and at the same time a reservoir of water."[12]
TR's related reclamation policy—to reclaim the arid areas of the West—
was closely linked with his conservation policy, helping to protect and
develop the nation's water supply.

Roosevelt's utilitarian approach to using natural resources to solid-
ify American power was coupled with an aesthetic appreciation of the
beauty of the outdoors, especially in special places like the Grand Canyon, which he visited in 1903, telling the local population:

> I want to ask you to do one thing in connection with it. In
> your own interest and the interest of all the country keep this
> great wonder of nature as it now is. I hope you won't have
> buildings of any kind to mar the grandeur and sublimity of
> the canyon. You cannot improve upon it. The ages have been
> at work on it, and man can only mar it. Keep it for your chil-
> dren and your children's children and all who come after you
> as one of the great sights for Americans to see.[13]

Continuing on his journey west to the Pacific Coast, he visited California and spent time camping in Yosemite National Park with the famous naturalist writer, John Muir (an outspoken critic of Gifford Pinchot's utilitarian approach, but he did not let disagreement with the administration's policy affect his friendship with TR). Filled with awe by the experience, he afterwards told the residents of Sacramento: "Lying out at night under those giant Sequoias was like lying in a temple built by no hand of man, a temple grander than any human architect could by any possibility build, and I hope for the preservation of the groves of giant trees simply because it would be a shame to our civilization to let them disappear. They are monuments in themselves."[14]

THE PELICAN ISLAND PRECEDENT

These experiences reinforced Roosevelt's determination to press ahead with his conservation agenda, which was expanded when he was informed that the brightly colored birds of Pelican Island, Florida, were being hunted for feathers to be used in women's hats and apparel. Disgusted at this slaughter, he was yet uncertain whether he could respond. "Is there any law that will prevent me from declaring Pelican Island a Federal Bird Reservation?" he wondered, and upon discovering there was none, said without another thought, "Very well, then I so declare it."[15]

His decision to create the nation's first federal wildlife refuge on Pelican Island was largely ignored by the newspapers but stands out as an advance of the conservation movement by expanding the president's power to establish wildlife sanctuaries on federal land. Following this precedent, he eventually declared fifty more areas under government protection during his administration, a broadminded policy that was followed by many presidents after him. By the end of the twentieth century, about four hundred federal wildlife refuges existed throughout the United States.

Some wonder why Roosevelt did not create more than five national parks. The answer: Congress, not the president, held this power, and political opposition in the legislature would often rise up and thwart his desires. To get around this obstacle, he championed the Antiquities Act, which gave him the power to sidestep Congress and create national monuments—he created sixteen of them; today there are 117—by presidential proclamation. In this manner he protected the Grand Canyon from commercial exploitation until Congress declared it a national park a decade later.

By convening the first Conservation Congress at the White House in 1908, he gave the conservation movement a prominence it had never enjoyed before. More than that, Roosevelt's balanced approach of aggressive conservation and preservation matched with generous, utilitarian stewardship of the nation's natural resources remains a model for conservative statesmen to follow today.

CHAPTER THIRTEEN

DELIVERING WATER TO THE ARID WEST

~

M ost Americans rightly praise Theodore Roosevelt for awakening the nation to the need to conserve its natural resources. Yet a related policy, which was just as important to the future development of the United States, has largely been forgotten: his foresight in bringing water to the arid parts of the West. Most of the millions of people who live in the former desert that stretches across the Southwest are oblivious to the fact that cities like Phoenix thrive because of his farsighted policy of making "reclamation" a centerpiece of his domestic agenda.

By the time Roosevelt reached the White House in 1901, practically nothing had been done to develop the dry areas of the West, most of which had been acquired as a result of the Mexican War a half century before. Private enterprise and local governments had undertaken small irrigation projects, but they were not equipped to construct the large water-supplying infrastructure that was needed. Only the federal government had resources sufficient to the immense task.

Unlike his predecessors in the White House, Roosevelt had a lively interest in the water-related challenges of West and set his mind on doing all he could to strengthen the long neglected region of the country, which to him was nothing less than "a magnificent empire"[1] in embryonic form. He wanted to help build up the West; he knew its development would enhance the strength of the United States on the global stage. He also had a personal affinity for the people of the region, believing they embodied the tough pioneer spirit that had built the country and that was necessary to keep it strong.

Roosevelt had lived in the West in the 1880s, spending sixteen months managing his cattle ranch in the Dakota territory. He became well acquainted then with the water-supply problem, having to quench the thirst of hundreds of cattle in the Badlands region susceptible to droughts so severe "a donkey could not live there." Despite this challenge, he was optimistic about the future of the area around his cattle ranch, writing in 1886 that parts of "Montana, and Wyoming, and the western strip of Dakota will bear the same relations to this country that Hungary does to Europe," where he said "a granger cannot subsist except on irrigated lands along the river."[2]

Realizing early on that irrigated lands would act as a magnetic force in attracting new settlers to the unpopulated areas of the West, he put the full weight of his administration behind legislation sponsored by Congressman Francis Newlands of Nevada (a member of the Boone and Crockett Club) in 1902 to create the federal Reclamation Service to help sixteen states and territories overcome their water-supply challenges. In backing Newlands, he was driven by a strong desire to expand development throughout the United States. He also knew support for the measure would elevate his high popularity in the West in the run-up to the 1904 presidential election and thereby help him win another term in the White House. His irrigation policy was therefore like many of his policies: both politically expedient and in the national interest.

Although Roosevelt's support for the Newlands Reclamation Act may have seemed self-serving, he defied his party in order to win its passage through Congress. Republicans from the East and Midwest, whose states would not benefit from government-backed irrigation because they already had an ample supply of water, opposed the plan as a costly boondoggle. The frugal Iowa Senator William Hepburn, for example, characterized the bill as "the most insolent attempt at larceny that I have ever seen in a legislative proposition." He was echoed by Joe Cannon, the Republican Speaker of the House, who declared, "I shall do whatever I can to defeat irrigation legislation."[3]

CONFOUNDING HIS CRITICS

In our own time, the complaints of fiscal hawks about excessive federal spending are reasonable in light of the nation's accumulated debt (now more than $18 trillion) and yearly deficits measured in hundreds of billion dollars. But during Roosevelt's administration the nation's balance sheet was healthy and strong, with a relatively small national debt and robust budget surpluses most years. The country was wealthy enough to afford to invest in infrastructure, and developing the West was, in Roosevelt's view, a national imperative. Giving perspective on the wealth of the United States in 1901, steel magnate Andrew Carnegie "calculated that America could afford to buy the entire United Kingdom, and settle Britain's national debt in the bargain."[4] Seen in this context and against the tremendous success of the Reclamation Service during the half century that followed, the opposition of provincial politicians like Hepburn and Cannon was shortsighted.

The Reclamation Service that President Roosevelt created with the stroke of a pen was hardly extravagant. It was, in effect, a federal loan program. Under its terms, states wishing to develop their water-supply infrastructure could ask the federal government to lend them money to build dams and aqueducts; they would then pay back the loan from the sale of land owned by the federal government in the affected territory. The promise of future irrigation would in turn boost the value of the land affected by the new water supply and thus increase the amount of revenue available to fund other projects. The engineers who ran the Reclamation Service managed the operation from Washington and decided which projects were feasible but otherwise did not impose an agenda on participating states.

Today's critics of Roosevelt might point to the Reclamation Act as another example of his alleged big government liberalism, but no less a conservative than Barry Goldwater, the five-term U.S. senator from Arizona from the 1950s to the 1980s, praised him for his role in transforming Phoenix into a major city:

> In Arizona we recently celebrated the 50th anniversary of the dedication of Theodore Roosevelt Dam.... The Theodore Roosevelt Dam is the key structure in the Salt River Project which brought a dependable water supply to 240,000 acres in central Arizona. This is the nation's first reclamation project. It has been tremendously successful and we locals do take pride in the accomplishment of our valley.... When the [Newlands Act] was passed and signed into law by President Theodore Roosevelt, the federal government, in effect, said to the people of Arizona: "We will not tell you where to build a dam, or what kind of dam to build. We will not organize your project. We will not dictate terms or conditions—resolve your differences among yourselves. Come to us with a proposal which will provide for the repayment of the funds you seek, plus interest, and if your project offers a reasonable guarantee of success, we will loan you some money.[5]

The thriving metropolitan area in and around Phoenix epitomizes the success of Roosevelt's irrigation policy, but it does not do justice to the scope of his triumph, which was achieved without burdening American taxpayers. By the mid-1980s, the Reclamation Service had exhausted most of the work that stood before it when it was created in 1902. Over that span of time, it invested roughly $8 billion to build out the water-supply infrastructure that makes life possible in many parts of the West, including the creation of:

- 700 dams
- 16,000 miles of aqueducts
- 35,000 miles of irrigation ditches
- 275 miles of water tunnels
- 241 pumping plants

If Roosevelt were alive today, he would undoubtedly smile at this amazing life-sustaining system that provides enough water "to flood Indiana under 12 inches of water" and "irrigate 9 million acres of land," enabling "55 million tons of food, fiber and forage" to be grown annually.[6] The Newlands Act received little attention when passed, yet one of the most conservative politicians in the country, Mark Hanna, realized its significance. "People have not paid much attention to this business," he said. "It's a damn big thing."[7]

Historians generally praise President Dwight Eisenhower for creating the Interstate Highway system, which binds the nation together via a network of roads; but Roosevelt's success in irrigating the Western desert has been largely ignored, though it is equally significant.

It is also worth comparing Theodore Roosevelt's development program with the programs initiated by Franklin Roosevelt during the New Deal. TR's goal embodied in the Reclamation Service was the long-term development of the United States using "bottom up" financing and decentralizing power outward to individual states, while the goal embodied in the Works Progress Administration (WPA) of FDR was the short-term stimulation of the economy using "top down" spending by the federal government.

When conservatives look for a historical figure to blame for the country's fiscal problems, they should point their fingers at Franklin Roosevelt, not his distant cousin Theodore, since Franklin was the first president to use massive government spending to stimulate a weak economy. Theodore Roosevelt was a man who believed in the pioneer spirit, not the all-wise bureaucrat.

CHAPTER FOURTEEN

WINNING—THEN LOSING—BLACK VOTERS

~

Theodore Roosevelt invited a black man, Booker T. Washington, to dinner at the White House, something that had never been done before. He also had a Jewish-American, Oscar Strauss, as a member of his Cabinet, as Secretary of Commerce and Labor. He deserves credit for these historic firsts, but his overall record on race relations is mixed. One can argue that Roosevelt could have done more to challenge racial injustice, but as a conservative statesman, he proceeded with caution.

Roosevelt was inaugurated as president only forty years after the start of the Civil War, the bloodiest war in American history. The strife, failure, and resentment that resulted from Reconstruction after the war, when the South was governed under martial law, was not a distant memory. In the 1870s the Democrat Party had begun its resurgence in the South, and by the 1890s it had erected a new system of segregation under so-called "Jim Crow" laws that often also left black citizens without voting rights. In 1896, the Supreme Court gave its constitutional approval to "separate but equal" segregation with its ruling in *Plessy v. Ferguson.*

While Roosevelt, as a Republican and an admirer of Abraham Lincoln, was sympathetic to the plight of black Americans, he concluded that the policy of Charles Sumner, Thaddeus Stevens, and the other "Radical Republicans" who dominated Congress during the Reconstruction era was wrongheaded; it prematurely gave the freed slaves political rights that they, he felt, were not ready to exercise. As he later wrote in a private letter, "the passage of the 15th Amendment at the time it was passed was a mistake" because it ignored the fact that blacks had only recently been slaves, and thus were unprepared to exercise political rights or power.[1]

His views were not outside the mainstream of public opinion, which largely opposed the idea that all blacks should have been given the suffrage after the Civil War. Indeed, he favored the policy of Abraham Lincoln, which was to permit "very intelligent Negroes and those who served our cause as soldiers" during the Civil War to vote.[2] As it was, Southern whites regarded the newly enfranchised and elected former slaves as ignorant tools of the Republican Party.

TR'S COMPLEX RACIAL ATTITUDES

Roosevelt's declaration that the Fifteenth Amendment was "unjust and bad policy"[3] grates against the inclusive sensibilities of our own time, as does the statement he made privately in 1906 to his friend Owen Wister: "Now as to the Negroes! I entirely agree with you that as a race and in the mass they are altogether inferior to the whites."[4] It is easy to cherry-pick quotes like these, as can be done with other historical figures (including Lincoln), to condemn TR as a racist. No doubt, he shared some of the prejudices common to Americans at the time. But that generalization fails to convey the larger truth: he wanted to help black Americans rise in American society, as he expressed in one of his most commendable sayings: "Our only safe motto is 'all men up' and not 'some men down.'"[5]

Like all educated people of his generation, Roosevelt was influenced by the intellectual currents of the day, including aspects of Social Darwinism that presumed that cultures, nations, and races had developed at different speeds. His generation also believed Western civilization, and its mainly white population, had advanced far ahead of the rest of the world in terms of military power, industrial might, higher learning, and technological innovation. Being his own man, Roosevelt noted deviations from the pattern, even condemning upper class white Americans for avoiding the Strenuous Life, a choice that signaled decadence and decline. He also saw a positive exception to this hierarchy: the Japanese, an alien people in far away Asia, had taken a giant leap upward in the world's pecking order during the second half of the nineteenth century by their rapid industrialization. As a result, the Land of the Rising Sun had joined the West on the top rung of the global power structure.

In treating Japan with respect and deference throughout his presidency, Roosevelt showed he cared more about power than race. He admired the Japanese; they were a strong, warlike people who had shown prowess in vying with the nations of Europe, even defeating one of them, Russia, in decisive fashion in a dramatic land and sea war that ended in 1905. At the other extreme, he looked at the Chinese with disdain; they had willingly surrendered to European domination. If TR were driven by racial prejudice, he would have lumped both of these Asian peoples together as inferior "yellow" races. Instead he elevated one to a level equal to his own people because it had developed into a world class power and posed a potential threat to American interests. Roosevelt believed black Americans, as a group, stood on a developmental rung above the Indians on the race ladder ("the Negro," he said, "unlike so many of the inferior races, does not dwindle away in the presence of the white man"[6]), yet his policy toward them was nonetheless similar, which was to try to help their advancements in education and every other aspect of American life. He was more optimistic about the ability of blacks to assimilate into white society given their development over the previous generation, telling Owen Wister: "My own personal belief is that the talk about the Negro having become worse since the Civil War is the veriest nonsense. He has on the whole become better."[7]

WINNING THE AFFECTIONS OF BLACKS AS GOVERNOR

Roosevelt's paternalism may rankle our modern sensibilities but nonetheless produced commendable actions in promoting racial harmony at a time when racism was rife throughout the United States and blacks endured blatant injustice in the South. As governor of New York, for instance, he won the hearts of black Americans everywhere when he pushed to fully integrate black children into the state's public schools. His policy was viewed so favorably by the nation's black community that a Baltimore newspaper declared in October 1900, "Governor Roosevelt is the popular idol of the colored people," adding:

> Since the publication in the news columns of many newspapers, including *The Sun*, that Governor Roosevelt had been especially active in securing the passage of a law in New York which obliterated every race distinction in the public schools, the colored people of Maryland and the South look upon the candidate as the coming "deliverer" of their race. "I am glad to know my own child sat in school with a Negro child," is one of Gov. Roosevelt's sayings that is passed along by the colored political leaders until nearly every Negro in Baltimore is aching to get out and shout for the Hero of San Juan Hill.[8]

With Roosevelt, political considerations could never entirely be put aside, but his personal interactions with black Americans were cordial and generous, respectful and kind, and full of a common decency that was less common than it should have been. When a well-known baritone named Burleigh sang in a private performance for the governor and afterwards could not book a hotel room in Albany because he was black, Roosevelt intervened, telling the baritone, "What's that! Here, Burleigh, you come with me. I'll see to it that you get a bed,"[9] and then invited him to spend the night at the Executive Mansion.

The fact that this incident became public could be justified by a governor wanting to set a good example, but Roosevelt's Democrat opponents argued it was simply politics, pandering to black voters, accusing TR of making sure "every Albany newspaper would announce the next morning that Mr. Burleigh had been a guest at the Executive Mansion."[10]

Though Blacks were disenfranchised in the segregated South, they continued to wield power within the Republican Party. Even in those Southern states where blacks could not vote in presidential elections because of Jim Crow laws, a small army of delegates came every four years to the Republican Party's presidential nominating convention.

William McKinley's campaign manager, Mark Hanna, locked up the support of Southern black delegates in the 1896 presidential election by bribing them with government jobs and other financial favors. Roosevelt, as governor, made a point of firming up his own party support among blacks by positioning himself as a Republican politician of progressive racial views.

DINING WITH BOOKER T. WASHINGTON

In October 1901, only a month after Vice President Roosevelt had become President Roosevelt, following McKinley's assassination, TR and his entire family hosted a dinner at the White House for Booker T. Washington, the most influential black American leader at the time. Although Roosevelt said he was surprised at the public furor that erupted after the dinner, no American president had ever dined with a black man as a social equal, and many newspapers and politicians in the South assumed no president ever should. The reaction of the *Memphis Commercial Appeal* was typical:

> *The Commercial Appeal* has always stood up for the rights
> of the Negro and expects to continue to do so. But the color

line must be drawn and drawn firmly when the social aspect
of the matter is considered. President Roosevelt has committed a blunder that is worse than a crime, and no atonement
or future act of his can remove the self-imprinted stigma.[11]

Infamous for his racist rhetoric, Senator "Pitchfork Ben" Tillman of
South Carolina went a step further with an ominous prediction: "The
action of President Roosevelt in entertaining that nigger will necessitate
our killing a thousand niggers in the South before they will learn their
place again."[12]

Roosevelt brushed aside these attacks as much ado about nothing.
He continued to have high regard for Booker T. Washington ("I do not
know a white man of the South who is as good a man as Booker Washington," he said[13]) and frequently asked for his help in identifying qual-
ified black candidates for federal jobs.

Historians usually portray the Booker T. Washington incident as an
example of Roosevelt's courage in defying the racial intolerance of white
Southerners. But he had more to gain than to lose: the "Solid South" was
a Democrat stronghold. Provoking the anger of white Southerners who
would never vote for him because he was a Republican was a small price
to pay for winning the support of nearly every black American who might
be inspired to cast a ballot in the North and West in the general election.

Roosevelt took pride in enforcing the law even when it was unpopular to do so, asserting as a U.S. Civil Service commissioner he would not
flinch from his duty. "I am a great believer in practical politics," he wrote
to Henry Cabot Lodge at the time, "but when my duty is to enforce a
law, that law is surely going to be enforced, without fear or favor. I am
perfectly willing to be turned out—or legislated out—but while in I mean
business."[14] Yet he did not take action to enforce the Fifteenth Amendment on Southern states that were violating it (and neither did any other
post-Reconstruction president until President Eisenhower attempted to
press the issue with his 1957 Civil Rights Act). This "do nothing" policy
of TR and other presidents de facto allowed white Southerners to use
Jim Crow laws and the threat of violent reprisals through the Ku Klux

Klan to keep blacks from casting ballots. In this, Roosevelt was apparently guided by "practical politics" after all, as dismantling segregation and enforcing the Fifteenth Amendment would likely have required a second military occupation of the Southern states—something that even the aggressive trust buster could not contemplate, as the domestic upheaval would have been enormous.

Historians have praised Roosevelt for making a few high-profile appointments of blacks in the South, when for example he nominated William Crum, M.D., to head of the Customs House in Charleston, South Carolina. This was one of the most coveted government jobs in the South; it infuriated white Southerners to see the position given to a black man whom they considered unqualified. To his credit, Roosevelt used a recess appointment to put Crum in the job against fierce political opposition. Later he was able to persuade a reluctant U.S. Senate to confirm the nomination.

It is true that in the first sixteen months of his administration, he appointed only thirteen blacks to roughly three thousand whites to federal jobs, which sounds like a modest number, but it is equally true that his appointments of black candidates were not the result of spoils politics, as McKinley's were. Certainly in the 1904 presidential election, Roosevelt could legitimately be positioned as a candidate who was a champion of black Americans.

MISHANDLING THE BROWNSVILLE INCIDENT

Only two years later, however, TR's immense popularity among blacks evaporated overnight when he discharged a regiment of black soldiers from the U.S. Army after they allegedly "shot up" the town of Brownsville, Texas, in August 1906. More than a century has passed since this incident took place; the details remain murky beyond the indisputable fact that a number of men moved through the town at night and fired into a number of houses, killing one person and wounding a few others. TR promptly ordered the U.S. Army to investigate the incident; the army determined

the black regiment stationed at Fort Brown, adjacent to Brownsville, per-
petrated the shooting because members of the unit had been mistreated
by the white residents of the area.

The army's report, however, failed to identify any specific soldiers
who had participated in the raid. Roosevelt responded with an ultimatum, telling the black soldiers at Fort Brown that if they did not come
forward and admit their culpability or inform on the guilty within their
ranks, he would dishonorably discharge all of them from the U.S. Army.
When no one confessed to the crime, he did exactly as he promised and
promptly discharged the men "without honor."

The action was kept relatively quiet until after the 1906 congressional elections, when it became public knowledge and an immediate
political firestorm erupted, with Roosevelt's critics, including many
blacks who had previously supported him, accusing him of committing
a grave injustice against the 167 black soldiers whom he summarily
discharged (on the advice of the Army inspector general). In public utter-
ances, TR had regularly stated his policy was to "treat each black man
and each white man strictly on his merits as a man, giving him no more
and no less than he shows himself worthy to have."[15] But in treating the
black regiment at Fort Brown as he did, he did not treat each black soldier
"on his merits as a man" as he promised to always do, but lumped them
all together as a group of guilty men engaged in a "conspiracy of silence,"
even though six of the discharged black soldiers had won the Congressional Medal of Honor for fighting Spaniards, Filipino insurrectionists,
and Indians.[16]

Roosevelt's apparent disregard for his own standard of justice might
have been driven by at least three factors: namely, the advice he was given
by the Army inspector general; his own innate preference for dramatic,
even peremptory action (he might have done exactly the same with an
accused white regiment; this was a man after all who had once threatened
to use the military to seize coal mines); and perhaps a calculation regarding public safety (would allowing the regiment to go unpunished trigger
further violence? It was certainly the case that racial animosity in the
South could be virulent. A terrible race riot had happened in Atlanta only

a month before, in September 1906, after newspaper accounts accused black men of threatening and assaulting white women).

Two years earlier Roosevelt had summed up his conservative approach to race relations in a letter to a political acquaintance, "the principal hope of the Negro must lie in the sense of justice and good will of the people in the South," adding, "the northern people can do but little for him."[17] But there were many who thought the president should have done much more to ensure that the Buffalo Soldiers of the 25th Infantry Regiment had received justice as individuals and were not merely scapegoated *en masse.*

In 1972, author John D. Weaver published his book, *The Brownsville Raid: The Story of America's Black Dreyfus Affair,* an exposé of how the men of the 25th Infantry Regiment had been summarily discharged "without honor" but also without one of them being found guilty of any charge. The book led Ronnie Dugger, the publisher of a black-owned newspaper, the *Texas Observer,* to declare: "Teddy Roosevelt committed one of the most blatant racist injustices in the history of our all-white Presidency."[18] This sentiment was shared by Congress, which soon passed legislation that President Richard Nixon signed into law that awarded $25,000 to each of the 167 soldiers who were still living (only one, it turned out) as reparation for the injustice.

DAMAGE TO THE PARTY OF LINCOLN

In 1906, the Republican Party enjoyed the strong support of the black community; that all changed after Roosevelt's Brownsville decision was announced in November of that year. The *New York Times* captured the reaction:

> Deep resentment over the action of President Roosevelt in discharging without honor three companies of the colored 25th United States Infantry was expressed yesterday by the preachers in the Negro churches of the city. They protested against the arbitrary nature of the order and declared that the President

never would have dared to give like treatment to white soldiers. They saw in the selection of a Southerner to make the official investigation into the troubles at Brownsville a truckling to sectional prejudice, and they declared in so many words that the Negroes of New York would seek revenge at the ballot box.... Rev. Dr. F. M. Jacobs said... "Theodore Roosevelt, once enshrined in our love as our Moses, now enshrouded in our scorn as our Judas."[19]

Blacks followed through on their threat to punish the Republican Party for Roosevelt's decision. In 1908—for the first time ever—they voted in large numbers for the Democrats, who that year ran William Jennings Bryan against William Howard Taft in the presidential election. Their movement away from the Republicans was made worse by the fact that Taft—the secretary of war at the time of the Brownsville incident—had agreed with Roosevelt's discharge order and promptly executed it. Taft won the election but the loss of black support commenced a long-term migration of black voters out of the party, which reached critical mass during the 1930s under President Franklin Roosevelt. Today, the Democrat candidate typically receives around 95 percent of the black vote in presidential contests. The erosion of black support for the Republican Party began with Theodore Roosevelt.

Roosevelt again stoked the anger of blacks when he refused to allow black delegates from the South to be recognized at the Bull Moose Party's convention in 1912. In the North, blacks and whites were mixed together in each state's delegation; in the South, whites refused to sit with their black peers, creating competing black and white delegations in each southern state. By agreeing to sit the white southern delegations but not the black ones, TR apparently hoped to win white support in the South (especially as whites were the only ones, as a practical matter, who could actually vote in the general election). But as a consequence, he convinced many blacks throughout the country that he was, as the black pastor F. M. Jacobs had declared two years earlier, a Moses turned into a Judas.

In defense of Roosevelt, his heart was in the right place, even if his political actions, at least regarding the Brownsville incident and the Bull Moose delegates, sometimes seemed to belie his words and his obvious cordial dealings with black Americans as individuals. He sincerely wanted to improve race relations but wanted even more to keep the country stable and peaceful. In his personal interactions with black Americans, he lived up to his principle of treating "every man on his merits as a man" and was known for his friendly manner with black chauffeurs and porters and others. But like many presidents before and after him, he turned away from a race problem in the South that he could not solve, and instead focused on issues that he could do something about. This was a wise choice in terms of practical politics. But his ill-considered action in the Brownsville affair, and the resulting loss of the black vote for the Republican Party over the next century, were moral and political failures of serious magnitude.

PART IV

TR AS

PRESIDENT:

FOREIGN

POLICY

1901 TO 1909

CHAPTER FIFTEEN

BRITAIN: FORGING THE SPECIAL RELATIONSHIP

~

B oth in his time and our own, Theodore Roosevelt's most enduring foreign-policy achievement has been overlooked, namely, the
way in which he fostered Anglo-American relations into a new
era of harmonious partnership. The warm bond of peace and friendship
that exists today between the United States and Great Britain has grown
so strong that it appears to be almost indestructible, giving the impression that the bond stretches all the way back to the end of the Revolutionary War (or the War of 1812). Others might cite a different origin,
remembering that Franklin Roosevelt and Winston Churchill forged an
unbreakable Anglo-American alliance in the 1940s to defeat Nazi Germany.

But the "Special Relationship" between the United States and Britain
(as Churchill affectionately called it) was not born at either point but
took root during the Spanish-American War. Up until that moment,
Anglo-American relations had been contentious for as long as anyone
could remember. At the Peace of Paris in 1783, Britain grudgingly

accepted U.S. independence but harbored hostility that lingered throughout the nineteenth century. During the Napoleonic wars, Britain used her powerful navy to assert dictatorial control over the seas in its effort to defeat France; she felt no moral qualms in seizing American ships and sailors to help achieve that end, even though these seizures violated international law. Britain's conduct was so outrageous, it pushed the United States—led at the time by a shy scholar, James Madison—into a rash declaration of war against the naval superpower of the age, which possessed fifty times as many warships as the miniscule U.S. Navy.

Surprisingly, the War of 1812 ended more or less in a draw between the mismatched contestants, a satisfactory outcome for the United States, yet the peace negotiated at Ghent resolved none of the issues that drove the budding republic to declare war in the first place. With old wounds continuing to fester, new resentments grew out of the bad war memories. Americans could not forget the burning of their nation's capital by pillaging Redcoats, and neither could the British forget the handful of startling naval defeats they had suffered at the hands of the small U.S. Navy.

After the war, the United States and Britain sank into heated commercial competition over emerging markets in South America, where a wave of popular revolutions created numerous new republics from Cape Horn to the Rio Grande. Not wanting to fall behind its English-speaking rival across the Atlantic, Britain in the 1820s quickly followed the United States in recognizing these new republics and acquiesced to the new Monroe Doctrine, formulated by John Quincy Adams. England simply saw the assertion of American power as an indirect way to protect British interests in South America from other European states.

As important as South American markets were to ensuring Britain's commercial dominance in the world, Canada represented a more vital territorial interest. The United States had invaded its northern neighbor during the Revolutionary War and the War of 1812; Britain understandably worried about the security of its colonial possession in North America as the power of the United States steadily grew during the nineteenth century. To make things worse, the boundary line west of the Mississippi

River between Canada and the United States had never been firmly established. That fluid situation provided the opportunity, if the United States desired, to expand into the empty spaces that would later become the Canadian provinces of Alberta and British Columbia, and thereby deny Britain land access to the Pacific Ocean from the North American continent.

After years of tough negotiations, Britain and the United States fixed the boundary line in the 1840s. This compromise agreement, in which President James Polk needlessly gave up a vast amount of territory in the Pacific Northwest, should have transformed Anglo-American relations and marked the beginning of lasting friendship between the two English-speaking nations. But Britain's fear of the United States as a growing threat to her interests continued unabated.

In the course of his voluminous historical writings, Theodore Roosevelt touched frequently on Anglo-American relations during the nineteenth century and noted the on-going hostility of Britain's government toward his country. By the late 1880s, he had visited London four times; on the whole, he came to like and admire the British people, but the conduct of the British government and educated class toward America angered him. He especially felt the sting of Britain's smug sense of superiority toward her former colonies, remembering that Charles Dickens, after a tour of the United States in the 1840s, had insulted Americans by declaring their country was "so maimed and lame, so full of sores and ulcers, foul to the eye and almost hopeless to the sense, that her best friends turned from the loathsome creature with disgust."[1]

PERSONAL FRIENDSHIPS LAY THE FOUNDATION

Always eager to defend his country against insults from condescending foreigners, Roosevelt was nevertheless friendly toward Britons who treated him with civility. While traveling on a steamship bound for Britain in 1886 to marry his second wife, Edith Carow, he met and befriended Cecil Spring-Rice, who was destined to become a leading

British diplomat. The two men formed such an immediate connection that Spring-Rice stood as the best man at the marriage ceremony at St. George's Church, Hanover Square. Afterwards, TR's new British friend took him around to the best clubs to meet the country's leading politicians. "His presence fills the room with an uninterrupted glow of smilingness," wrote one newspaper describing how the twenty-eight-year-old TR took London by storm, noting, "Mr. Roosevelt's table in Brown's Hotel is covered with invitations to four times as many dinners as he can eat, and to any number of jolly things. He hunts the fox in Essex on Monday and is put up at the Athenaeum Club."[2]

Roosevelt was more than socializing during his honeymoon; he was also building a large network of contacts with influential Britons, starting with Spring-Rice and expanding until it eventually included dozens of statesmen and men of letters. His magnetic, charismatic personality helped attract other men to him. As a London newspaper noted: "The men here like Roosevelt, and he knows it. He thinks it is because he is thoroughly American.... Englishmen, he says, respect those who do not imitate them, which is true, and which is something many Americans have yet to learn."[3]

Thrilled at all the attention, TR forgot Britain's history of antipathy toward the United States and gushed over his new British friends:

> The charm of London lies in the fact that there we meet men
> who know how to have a good time and yet play their parts
> in the world. It is pleasant to stay at the country house of a
> mighty Nimrod who is also a prominent factor in politics, to
> meet men of note at the clubs, and to discuss art and literature
> at a dinner where there are leaders of Parliament in addition
> to leaders of fashion.[4]

An American through and through, Roosevelt was nonetheless, as many upper class Americans were, British in many of his values and attitudes, which opened doors into the inner circles of power in London.

No American president before or since has had so many personal contacts in Europe—not even John Quincy Adams, who lived for twenty-two years on the continent as a U.S. diplomat and yet made no lasting friendships with Europeans. Unlike the misanthropic Adams, the extrovert Roosevelt returned to the United States in 1887 with an extensive list of names and addresses of men he would correspond with for the rest of his life; at the top of the list was his best man, Cecil Spring-Rice, who would later become Britain's ambassador to the United States during William Howard Taft's (starting in 1912) and Woodrow Wilson's administrations. Roosevelt and Spring-Rice saw each other often during the early 1890s, when Roosevelt lived in Washington as a U.S. Civil Service commissioner and Spring-Rice served as a diplomat at the British Embassy. They became very close friends; the personal bond they developed was as important as that which Franklin Roosevelt and Winston Churchill developed fifty years later in forging the Special Relationship between the United States and Britain.

The lifelong correspondence between Roosevelt and Spring-Rice strikingly projects the trust and intimacy between them, especially when Roosevelt served in the White House and carefully guarded the secrets of his administration. While four other men served as Britain's ambassador in Washington during Roosevelt's presidency, none enjoyed the special access that Spring-Rice did even though he was posted elsewhere. Roosevelt wrote Spring-Rice lengthy letters on foreign affairs, treating him de facto as Britain's ambassador, as well as a friend.

THE CRISIS OF 1895:
BRITAIN BACKS DOWN

However close Roosevelt was to Spring-Rice and other English friends, he knew the contentious history of Anglo-American relations as few Americans did, and believed that Britain, like the United States, would pursue her national interests. When a crisis erupted between the two nations in 1895, he put his friendships to the side, remarking, "a couple of centuries hence we may all be in one great federation, but just at present the Englishman is a foreigner and nothing else."[5] The crisis in Anglo-American relations that year involved a disputed boundary line in South America between Venezuela and Britain's colony of Guiana. The United States wanted the dispute to be settled through arbitration, but Britain refused, claiming a sovereign right to territory also claimed by Venezuela. Fearful Britain would use military force to assert its claim, President Grover Cleveland addressed Congress and made a bellicose declaration, publicly informing the British government that such action would represent a direct violation of the Monroe Doctrine and as a consequence would be resisted by American military force.

Motivated by the war drums beating in the White House, Roosevelt imagined himself donning a soldier's uniform and engaging in an American ground invasion of Canada. Writing to his brother-in-law, he gushed enthusiasm:

> I earnestly hope our government doesn't back down. If there is a muss I shall try to have a hand in it myself! They'll have to employ a lot of men just as green as I am even for the conquest of Canada. Our regular army isn't big enough. It seems to me that if England were wise she would fight now. We couldn't get at Canada until May, and meanwhile she could play havoc with our coast cities and shipping.[6]

He must have felt disappointed when he heard the news that Lord Salisbury, head of Britain's government, had backed down in the face of Cleveland's ultimatum, reluctantly accepting arbitration to resolve the dispute peacefully. The resolution of the Venezuela crisis represented a diplomatic defeat for Britain; but for Lord Salisbury, the epitome of a conservative statesman, it represented simple pragmatism and prudence. Britain had little to gain—in the event, about ninety percent of the disputed territory was awarded to Britain anyway by the Tribunal of Arbitration in 1899—and much to lose in a costly war in a faraway colony. Salisbury also had his eye on Germany, a rapidly growing power with an increasingly bellicose foreign policy under the leadership of the unpredictable Kaiser Wilhelm II. The British prime minister saw no reason to increase Britain's number of enemies by antagonizing the United States, and Britain actually tacitly supported America in the Spanish-American War in 1898.

Roosevelt was delighted by the shift in British policy. After he became governor of New York he said:

> I used to be rather anti-British in feeling and when President Cleveland's Venezuela message went into the Senate I promptly applied for a command at the War Department just as I afterward did in the war with Spain, but England's attitude toward us in our war with Spain impressed me deeply and I have ever since kept it in lively and grateful remembrance.[7]

During the Spanish-American War Germany and Russia had been hostile to the United States and tried to arrange a peace conference to settle the conflict, presumably in Spain's interest. Britain refused to participate, not wanting to undermine American foreign policy. While Britain was officially neutral during the Spanish-American War, she repeatedly demonstrated support for the United States—and such diplomatic support continued after the war.

DEFERRING TO U.S. INTERESTS IN CENTRAL AMERICA

Under the Clayton-Bulwer Treaty of 1850, the United States and Britain had agreed to a partnership arrangement as regards a future canal through Central America connecting the Caribbean Sea with the Pacific Ocean. During the McKinley administration, both countries sat at the negotiation table to replace the old treaty with an updated agreement that recognized new conditions—chiefly America's interest to take action on its own and Britain's acceptance of the Monroe Doctrine as being in the interests of both countries. By the time Roosevelt became president, Britain had agreed to surrender control of the future canal to the United States and, in November 1901, the countries accordingly signed the Hay-Pauncefote Treaty. It was a

decidedly one-sided deal in America's favor and recognized as such by the
U.S. Senate, which ratified the pact by an overwhelming 72-to-6 vote.

The Hay-Pauncefote Treaty enabled the United States to build the
Panama Canal without interference, but its diplomatic significance lay
in tightening the bonds of friendship between the United States and
Britain. By surrendering its rights to the canal, Britain obtained the larger
strategic goal of securing American good will. Meanwhile, the rest of
Europe thoroughly enjoyed the spectacle of the mighty British Empire
apparently surrendering to the diplomatic demands of its former colonial
possession. The French newspaper *Journal des Debats* declared in a
barbed editorial: "The submission of England is as complete as the
American Senate could wish. It is interesting to again note that England
cannot live at peace with the United States except at the cost of perpetual
concessions and sacrifices."[8] The jingo element in the British press agreed,
howling in rage, "British rights on the isthmus have been abandoned
without a tangible equivalent" and that if such a policy continued "it will
not be long before Great Britain is invited to surrender the West Indies
and even Canada as peace offerings to American chauvinism."[9]

The conservative *London Times* offered a soberer perspective, seeing
the Hay-Pauncefote Treaty not as an obsequious surrender to the United
States but rather a wise "closing of a controversy which has been used
for a long time past to prevent the growth of good feeling between the
United States and the British Empire." It pointed out, "The immense
increase of the power of the United States on the American continent
during the last half century and the rapidly developing possibilities of
American trade have materially changed the aspect of the question." The
Times congratulated the British government for its willingness "to con-
cede everything except essential and practical interests to the altered
wishes and expanded aspirations of a friendly nation."[10]

When Roosevelt arrived in the White House, he received a gift that
no other American president had ever received: Britain, the world's greatest power, extending her hand to the United States in the sincere hope of
building a lasting friendship between the two English-speaking peoples.
To his credit, he reached out and grasped that hand with gusto, creating

a warm bond between the United States and Britain that endures to this day. As a hardnosed practitioner of *realpolitik*, TR knew Britain's decision to support the United States during the Spanish-American War and relinquish her rights to a canal in Central America was driven by the rising threat of Germany. He also understood the emergence of the United States as a world power was a big factor, telling a group of British journalists in 1910:

> It is a very pleasant thing to me, and I am sure to all of you here tonight, that the relations of the United States and England have grown so much better, and I want to call attention to this, that they have grown almost in proportion as the United States has grown stronger and less sensitive to what is said of it from outside. I am quite serious in saying that, so far from the growth of the United States being—as many of your statesmen once supposed would be the case—a menace to England, the chances of trouble to England from the United States have dwindled steadily in exactly inverse proportion to the growth of the strength of the United States.[11]

He, too, worried about Germany, a geographically distant power but possessing a large enough navy to carve out colonies in South America, a threat that would only increase unless the expansion of the American navy kept pace with Germany's massive shipbuilding effort. As early as 1897, he said privately, "Germany is the power with which we may very possibly have ultimately to come into hostile contact," adding, with disappointment that his countrymen did not see the same thing: "How I wish our people would wake up to the need for a big navy!"[12]

MASTER DIPLOMACY

Roosevelt's worries were exacerbated by another trend negative to American interests. As the German threat increased, Britain was showing signs of exhaustion in managing her vast empire. An insurrection among the Dutch Boers had flared up in South Africa, and Britain had difficulty extinguishing it. Watching from afar, Roosevelt marveled at the tenacious Boer resistance to British rule, seeing in it the warrior strength that he valued. He was sympathetic to the Boer cause, but believed their defeat was essential if South Africa was to become "a great commonwealth where the Dutch and English shall mingle just as they have mingled in New York."[13] Even as he remained the quintessential American patriot, he nonetheless believed it would be a "disaster to the civilized world and progress of mankind if the British Empire were to lose its strength."[14]

Maintaining strict neutrality just as his predecessor President McKinley had with regard to the South African war, Roosevelt was nonetheless tempted to make public statements in favor of the Boers but did not, recognizing the recent gestures of friendship from Britain needed to be reciprocated by silence from the American government. He was proud of his own Dutch ancestry and must have felt a tinge of guilt when Boer leaders called on him "with a certain dignified sorrow" because he "seemed to have no sympathy with them."[15]

He placated Britain with regard to her South African war but proved less flexible when it came to the Alaskan boundary dispute, which involved a narrow strip of territory along the Pacific Ocean. Twenty years before, maps had shown this land as American. But Canada challenged the claim, pressing the matter with her mother country (at the time, Britain still managed Canada's foreign policy). Believing the American claim was absolutely legitimate, TR refused to give an inch of land (land that was believed to harbor gold) and backed up his position with the threat of force. In 1902, he ordered his Secretary of War Elihu Root to send U.S. troops to the disputed area.

Fearful the Alaskan boundary dispute might produce a serious rupture in the burgeoning Anglo-American friendship, Roosevelt agreed to arbitration—but only to allow Canada to save face. He had no intention of allowing an arbitration panel to rule against the United States, and stacked it with Americans (including his closest friends Henry Cabot Lodge and Elihu Root), ordering them not to offer any compromises. The Canadians protested these appointments, with Sir Wilfrid Laurier, the high commissioner of Canada, pointing out in understated fashion that it seemed "anomalous that Mr. Root, a member of the administration of President Roosevelt, and therefore one of the suitors in the case, should sit on the bench as a judge."[16] Condemned by the *London Times* as a "heads I win, tails you lose" arrangement,[17] the arbitration of the boundary dispute was an American diplomatic victory of the first order, even if it was won against an opponent, Britain, which had already tacitly ceded Canada's claims, judging friendship with America more important.

Just as the Alaskan boundary dispute was being resolved in late 1903, the Colombian province of Panama erupted in revolution, declaring its independence. Roosevelt promptly recognized Panama as a new nation, dispatched American gunboats to protect it, and had a treaty negotiated and ratified, paving the way for the construction of the Panama Canal. Some observers in the United States condemned Roosevelt for breathing life into the new Panamanian republic, but the British government offered no criticism, declaring the events in Panama were "entirely the United States' affair."[18]

The *London Times*, the mouthpiece of Britain's ruling establishment, gave a more definitive verdict, editorializing, "the United States had a powerful and perfectly logical case in the matter" and that the policy of the Roosevelt administration "secures for the United States the power to create at last that great agency of universal commerce, the isthmian canal."[19] A year later, as Roosevelt exulted over his victory in the 1904 presidential election, the English politician John Morley visited him in the White House and "prophesied that the United States would be the greatest power on earth in the coming time." "There is not," Morley said, "a power in Europe that does not covet the friendship of the United States."[20] As did the British government, obviously.

SEALING THE TIES THAT BIND

By the time Roosevelt left the White House, diplomatic relations between the United States and Great Britain were stronger than they had ever been. The British politician Joseph Chamberlain spoke for many Britons when he declared in 1902 that President Roosevelt was "a very great man."[21] British statesmen, and the British people, had come to see the United States as a partner rather than a rival in global affairs. Roosevelt's diplomatic use of America's growing power paid *realpolitik* dividends.

Roosevelt's friendship with influential Britons also played an important role in cementing the Special Relationship. He corresponded for many years not only with his close friend Cecil Spring-Rice, but with the historian George Trevelyan, the politician John Morley, the scholar James Bryce, the diplomat Edward Grey, the aristocrat Arthur Lee, and numerous others among Britain's governing class. During his presidency, he invited many of these British friends to Washington and to stay with his family at the White House.

British respect for Roosevelt was matched by his admiration for Britain's empire, the largest empire in history. Before leaving the White House, he delivered a notable speech praising Britain's rule over India as not only "the most colossal example history affords of the successful administration by men of European blood of a thickly populated region in another continent" but also "the greatest feat of the kind that has been performed since the break-up of the Roman Empire."[22] Frequently criticized by her enemies as a harsh imperial power, Britain could not help but love an American president who publicly gushed over her achievements and who, after leaving the White House, spent a year hunting big game in her colonial possessions in East Africa. Roosevelt spent much of 1909 in Egypt, Sudan, and present-day Kenya. When he wasn't shooting big game, he charmed Britain's colonial administrators in the region. Far from acting as a harsh colonial power, Roosevelt thought Britain was too forbearing and needed to rule her colonies with a stronger hand, saying bluntly during his speech at London's Guildhall in 1910 that she should "govern or get out."

"In Egypt," he said, "weakness, timidity, and sentimentality may cause even more far-reaching harm than violence and injustice. Of all the broken reeds, sentimentality is the most broken reed on which righteousness can lean."[23] In Britain, his speech was taken with dignified grace, as advice offered by a friend. Some American newspapers were more scornful, accusing him, of trying to "make an impression in America of his boldness and wisdom as bearder of the British lion and trainer of the stupid beast."[24]

World War I solidified in Roosevelt's mind that Britain and the United States were bound to be long-term allies. In 1911, when William Howard Taft proposed that Britain and the United States could safely arbitrate any future disputes between them, Roosevelt was fiercely opposed to the idea. But after the United States and Britain had fought side by side in the trenches against Germany in World War I, he changed his mind. In December 1918, two months before his death, he wrote:

> I am now prepared to say what five years ago I would not have said. I think the time has come when the United States and the British Empire can agree to a universal arbitration treaty. In other words, I believe that the time has come when we should say that under no circumstances shall there ever be a resort to war between the United States and the British Empire, and that no question can ever arise between them that cannot be settled in judicial fashion in some such manner as questions between states of our own Union would be settled.... There are many countries not yet at a level of advancement which permits real reciprocity of relations between them, and many other countries so completely unlike our own that at present no such agreement would be possible with them. But the slow march forward of the generations has brought the English speaking peoples to a point where such an agreement is entirely feasible, and it is eminently desirable among ourselves.[25]

Roosevelt deserves a high grade for his work in forging a lasting Anglo-American partnership. There is no way his predecessor in the White House, William McKinley—a provincial politician who knew every boss in the Republican Party but practically nothing about European politics—could have built the special relationship between the United States and Britain with the expertise, finesse, and staying power that Roosevelt did.

CHAPTER SIXTEEN

GERMANY: RESTRAINING THE KAISER

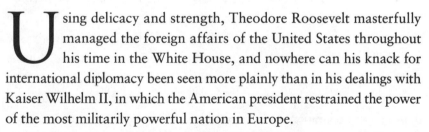

U sing delicacy and strength, Theodore Roosevelt masterfully managed the foreign affairs of the United States throughout his time in the White House, and nowhere can his knack for international diplomacy been seen more plainly than in his dealings with Kaiser Wilhelm II, in which the American president restrained the power of the most militarily powerful nation in Europe.

From the time of America's Founding, the American and German peoples had enjoyed peaceful relations. John Quincy Adams served as U.S. minister to Prussia during his father John Adams's administration (he had been nominated by then-president George Washington and continued to serve for two months under President Thomas Jefferson) and negotiated a commercial treaty with the Prussians in the 1790s. German-American ties were both commercial and personal, as many Americans in the eighteenth and nineteenth century were descended from German immigrants. After the unification of Germany under Prince Bismarck in the early 1870s, the two countries got along as harmoniously as they had before. America continued its diplomatic tradition of avoiding entanglements in European affairs and Germany and the United States had no serious conflicting interests elsewhere in the world.

This amiable state of affairs changed, however, when Germany acquired colonies, and subsequently began to build a large navy to defend them and its burgeoning commercial interests in Asia, Africa, and the Pacific. By 1898, the German navy had become a powerful weapon of war, matching the fighting strength of the U.S. Navy, and falling behind only those of Britain, France, and Russia in terms of size.[1] Now able to project military power into distant parts of the world and still hungry to acquire more colonies, Germany suddenly threatened American interests in the Western Hemisphere.

In 1898 the United States had won two impressive naval battles during its war with Spain, smashing Spanish fleets in Cuba and the Philippines. As brilliantly as the U.S. Navy performed against Spain—a declining old-world relic that had wielded little real power since the sixteenth century—it remained to be seen whether American forces could perform as well against a stronger, more modern navy like that of Germany, a rising power whose economy was booming and whose bellicose government, dominated by Prussian militarists and the mercurial Kaiser Wilhelm II, was eager to make an indelible mark on history. The United States had proclaimed the Monroe Doctrine in the 1820s, warning European nations it would no longer allow them to acquire territory in the Western Hemisphere. But this was little more than a paper declaration. As Roosevelt said on many occasions, the Monroe Doctrine was "as strong as the United States navy, and no stronger."[2] Despite Britain's Royal Navy being the power that "ruled the waves," Roosevelt believed that "Germany, and not England, is the power with whom we are most apt to have trouble over the Monroe Doctrine."[3]

Germany—unlike Britain, which already owned the world's greatest empire—was not a "satisfied" power; it was hungry to gain territory. Roosevelt understood that. He noted:

If I were a German I would want the German race to expand. I should be glad to see it begin to expand in the only two places left for the ethnic, as distinguished from the political, expansion of the European peoples, that is in South Africa and temperate South America. Therefore, as a German I should be delighted to upset the English in South Africa, and to defy the Americans and their Monroe Doctrine in South America.[4]

Roosevelt and Henry Cabot Lodge, his close friend and a Republican Senator from Massachusetts with a deep interest in foreign policy, worried that the weak nations of South America were a tempting target for European powers that wanted more colonies. TR argued that the United States had to "be dominant in the western hemisphere and keep it free from foreign invasion" rather than "let it be seized as Africa had been."[5]

The likelihood of a Panama Canal being constructed added to the strategic value of Latin America. Once the canal was built, a foreign power operating from a Central or South American colony could try to prevent other powers from using what would be a vital transit route between the Atlantic and Pacific oceans. Warships, which at the time relied on steam power generated by coal, had limited range. With refueling at sea by other ships a difficult task, the possession of a coaling station on land was a necessity if a navy wished to operate in geographically distant waters. A German colony in South America would be of immense value as a coaling station to refuel the German navy, allowing it to operate more easily in the Western Hemisphere.

INVITING GERMAN MISCHIEF IN SOUTH AMERICA

The apparent willingness of the United States to go to war against Britain during the Venezuelan crisis slowed Germany's ambitions in South America. But its deterrent effect evaporated in an instant when President Roosevelt opened the door to European interference in the region in his First Message to Congress in 1901 when he declared: "We do not guarantee any [South American] state against punishment [from

European powers] if it misconducts itself, provided that punishment does not take the form of the acquisition of territory by any non-American power."[6] The statement was one of the blunders of his presidency, as it opened up a Pandora's box of new problems, ultimately leading to his misguided decision to expand the Monroe Doctrine by adding a "police" power.

Seeing the Roosevelt administration had now given European powers permission to punish misbehaving South American states, Germany, through its ambassador in Washington, promptly notified the United States it would send a naval squadron to Venezuela in order to collect $2 million owed to German subjects by the country's government. To ease American fears about a possible infringement of the Monroe Doctrine, the ambassador emphasized that under no circumstances would Germany attempt to permanently acquire any territory.[7] Surprisingly, the U.S. government made no objection to this extraordinary plan. The news caused barely a ripple of interest in the press, with one newspaper reporting, "There is not the slightest feeling of uneasiness in Washington over the Venezuelan affair."[8]

We know President Roosevelt was concerned about the German naval expedition but decided to keep silent until it arrived in Venezuelan waters. The full story of the tense affair was not publicly known for another fifteen years. When finally told, the story revealed that both countries arrived at the brink of war, in large part because Roosevelt did not trust the German kaiser to leave Venezuela as he had promised. The secret diplomatic crisis began in December 1902 when a German fleet sailed into the Venezuelan harbor at La Guaira, sank a few of the country's gunboats, and then bombarded a fortress at Puerto Cabello, which guarded the harbor. Roosevelt must have winced when he heard the news. He had been informed by the German government its fleet would only enforce a "peace blockade" to coerce Venezuela to pay its debt,[9] but that promise had now been broken with military action that verged on a direct violation of the Monroe Doctrine.

"A bad impression has been created in this country by the events of the last two days in Venezuela," wrote the *London Times*. "What is objected to is the sinking of Venezuelan warships, which gives the expedition a punitive character."[10] Unable to contain his anger, Roosevelt summoned the German ambassador and asked for a definitive statement as to how long Germany would enforce its "peace blockade." When the ambassador declined to answer, the president told him that he could not let the affair go any further and insisted Germany agree to end its blockade and have the dispute settled by an arbitration tribunal.

TR ISSUES AN ULTIMATUM

When the ambassador answered that his government would not consent to this alternative, Roosevelt issued an ultimatum, telling him that unless Germany agreed to arbitration within ten days, he would send Admiral Dewey (famous for his seizure of Manila during the Spanish-American War) and the entire U.S. fleet to Venezuela to safeguard American interests. The ambassador said such action would produce something too frightening to name, and Roosevelt replied, "If it means war, you have chosen the one spot where you can't fight us."[11] To emphasize his seriousness, TR pulled out a map and showed the close proximity of Venezuela to the United States compared to far away Germany, which had no coaling stations near the Caribbean Sea.

A week later the German ambassador returned to the White House and informed the president that his government still refused to arbitrate the dispute. Seeing he had not been taken seriously, Roosevelt reiterated his ultimatum and moved the deadline up a day, announcing that in forty-eight hours he would send the order to Dewey to move the massive U.S. fleet, comprising more than fifty warships and every American battleship then afloat, to Venezuelan waters. A day later, the ambassador returned to inform the president that Germany would arbitrate.

Roosevelt kept the American people in the dark about his ultimatum. After Germany agreed to arbitration, he took pains to ensure that news of the diplomatic showdown did not leak out to the newspapers. He had delivered the ultimatum completely on his own authority without seeking advice from his Cabinet; he wanted to keep the controversy secret because he believed the kaiser would be more likely to back down if the eyes of the world were not upon him. He also wanted to avoid humiliating the proud German leader, which he knew would cause irreparable long-term damage to relations between the United States and Germany if the kaiser was ridiculed as a weakling in English, French, and American newspapers.

Roosevelt deserves immense credit for handling the affair discreetly, sacrificing the opportunity to bolster his own image as a military leader in order to protect the long-term interests of the United States. But the manner in which he stepped back from the promise he made in his 1901 Annual Message to Congress to permit European nations to punish misbehaving South American states, by abruptly issuing a secret ultimatum a year later, nearly took the United States into a war against one of Europe's great powers. He did not foresee the negative consequences of his initial policy, which had encouraged the kaiser's ambitions in South America.

The peaceful resolution of the Venezuelan crisis was a triumph for Roosevelt: the kaiser harbored no bitter feelings and indeed grew to like, trust, and admire the American president. Roosevelt's regard for the kaiser grew as well. In 1897 he had told a friend, "I am by no means sure that I heartily respect the little Kaiser."[12] But after dealing with him as a head of state, his opinion changed.

Newspapers often ridiculed the German leader as a preening militarist, but Roosevelt had come to believe the kaiser was "a powerful and able man"[13] of exceptional ability. When a visitor to the White House expressed surprise that the president possessed line drawings made personally by the kaiser showing in detail every ship in the U.S. Navy, he replied: "The Kaiser is a most extraordinary fellow, and not everyone realizes how extraordinary. He and I have corresponded ever since I became President, and I tell you that if his letters were ever published they would bring on a world war."[14]

He and the kaiser got along well in part because the two men shared a similar governing philosophy that emphasized military strength, or as H. L. Mencken succinctly put it, "the America that Roosevelt dreamed of was always a sort of swollen Prussia, truculent without and regimented within."[15] By the end of his first term in office he had become the kaiser's therapist, receiving letters from the German leader filled with paranoid fears that Britain was "planning to attack him and smash his fleet." Amused at these missives, he joked with his Secretary of State John Hay, "the Kaiser has become a monomaniac about getting into communication with me every time he drinks three penny's worth of conspiracy against his life and power," when in truth the British were "themselves in a condition of panic terror lest the Kaiser secretly intend to form an alliance against them with France or Russia, or both, to destroy their fleet and blot out the British Empire from the map!"[16]

COOLING TENSIONS AT ALGECIRAS

Roosevelt could laugh at the mutual mistrust between Germany and Britain but also felt concern it might boil into war. Tensions between the two countries skyrocketed after Britain and France signed a treaty in April 1904, which recognized and delineated Anglo-French spheres of influence in North Africa. By its terms, France gave Britain a free hand in governing Egypt and the Sudan while Britain acquiesced to French control of Morocco. The kaiser made no objections when this Anglo-French treaty was signed, but the balance of power in Europe suddenly shifted when France's ally Russia suffered a catastrophic defeat in Asia after its fleet was destroyed by Japan in May 1905. Seeing that Russia was now less likely to support France, the kaiser abruptly reversed his policy and challenged the validity of the Anglo-French treaty. He traveled to Tangiers and delivered a bellicose speech declaring that Germany would not acquiesce in French rule of Morocco, demanding that an international conference be held to resolve the controversy.

Realizing their attendance at this conference would mean Germany had effectively nullified their recent treaty of understanding, Britain and France refused the kaiser's demand. The resulting crisis could have triggered World War I eight years before it actually began had not President Roosevelt intervened. A firm believer in maintaining the balance of power in Europe, which included accepting legitimate spheres of influence, he immediately dismissed the kaiser's Moroccan initiative as nothing more than a "pipe dream."[17] Nonetheless, he concluded that the "altogether too jumpy and erratic" German leader might act rashly and trigger war in Europe if not handled with care.[18]

Accordingly, he told the French government through its ambassador in Washington he thought it "eminently wise" that France attend the conference to allow the kaiser to "save his face."[19] Roosevelt knew the kaiser would feel humiliated if the conference he championed were rejected out of hand (Germany had already itself refused a French offer of direct negotiations between the two powers). TR also assumed that if France agreed to attend, so would Britain.

Brilliant diplomacy was needed to persuade a proud and fearful French government to swallow its pride, but Roosevelt was up to the task. Always a shrewd negotiator, he pointed out that Britain could do little to help France in the event of war since Germany's invasion would come by land and not by sea. He also noted that the likely conference attendees would be decidedly pro-French. As such, Germany's diplomatic position would be undercut and Germany would be in no position to justify military action against France. He made clear that the United States would not attend the conference unless France first agreed to go. Bolstered by the unspoken yet clear message that the United States supported the French position, France finally yielded and agreed to attend the conference. Britain, not wanting to take a stand against its ally and the United States, quickly followed France's lead. Had Roosevelt not intervened in the dispute when he did, France and Britain likely would have stood firm in their refusal to resolve the Moroccan controversy in an international forum. Moreover, the "jumpy and erratic" kaiser, humiliated before the eyes of the world, might easily have then escalated the crisis into a full-blown war.

Biographers of Roosevelt inevitably focus on his diplomatic tour de force in negotiating an end to the Russo-Japanese War as it was the main reason why he won a Nobel Peace Prize. But his skillful use of diplomacy to bring the intractable antagonists in the Moroccan dispute together was arguably a larger achievement because the stakes were much higher. Had the conflict between Russia and Japan continued, many more lives would have been lost; yet those losses would hardly have compared to a full-blown war in Europe. Not only did Roosevelt persuade France—and indirectly, Britain—to humor the kaiser's call for an international conference, but once the conference began at Algeciras, Spain, Roosevelt broke a resulting diplomatic logjam and made a negotiated settlement possible.

By the time the Algeciras Conference opened in early 1906, Roosevelt had become convinced "Germany was aiming in effect at the partition of Morocco, the very reverse of what she was claiming to desire."[20] The kaiser insisted Germany be allowed to control a Moroccan port, and that another be given to Holland or Switzerland, which he assumed would eventually come under German control. With Germany's "peace blockade" of Venezuela in 1902 fresh in his mind, TR believed the kaiser was now using a similar ploy to pursue larger ambitions against France and Britain. When the conference bogged down into a dangerous stalemate that threatened to explode into war, the president decided once again to take an active role in bringing the antagonists together.

Communicating through the German ambassador in Washington, he informed the kaiser that if he did not accept the American plan for resolving the dispute, which involved giving control of all Moroccan ports to France and Spain, he would publish the full diplomatic correspondence between the United States and Germany regarding the dispute and thereby show the world that Germany was to blame for the stalemate. Adding a carrot to this stick, he indicated he would praise Germany for lofty statesmanship if it yielded its demands. A few days later, the Kaiser agreed to the American plan, effectively ending the Algeciras Conference. Although the United States had no direct interests in the European dispute, other than ensuring the "Open Door" to its commerce with Morocco was maintained, Roosevelt was the driving force that ensured the conference took place and ended without triggering a European war.

Discreet as ever, Roosevelt kept the details of his behind-the-scenes diplomatic maneuvers hidden from the public but wrote a long "posterity letter" to the U.S. ambassador in Britain, Whitelaw Reid, describing the course of events so that historians would know what actually happened. Soon a front-page story appeared in the *Chicago Tribune* under the large headline: "Peace in Europe Due to Roosevelt, Solution of Moroccan Problem Adds Biggest Feather to President's Diplomatic Cap, World Again His Debtor."[21]

No American president had ever used personal diplomacy with such effectiveness to restrain a dangerous foreign leader as Roosevelt did with the kaiser. It was a masterful performance based on a combination of trust, understanding, personal ties, and power politics that could be used by any president as a lesson in effective diplomacy.

CHAPTER SEVENTEEN

JAPAN:
PREVENTING WAR
IN THE PACIFIC

~

E very spring, thousands of tourists stroll along the tidal basin in
Washington to admire the spectacular beauty of the Japanese
cherry blossom trees as they emerge from winter dormancy. Few
among these flora-loving sightseers realize they owe Theodore Roosevelt
a debt of gratitude for the experience. At the beginning of the last century, when Russia and Japan were embroiled in a war in Asia, he stepped
between the two countries and ended the conflict. He won the Nobel
Peace Prize for this achievement and another trophy for his country: the
cherry blossom trees, which were given to the United States as a token
of thanks from the mayor of Tokyo for Roosevelt's peacemaking.

Relations between the two nations were not always this close. Insu-
lar and xenophobic, Japan closed itself off from the Western world until
1853 when Commodore Matthew Perry convinced the Japanese to trade
with the United States. In the decades that followed, Japan gradually
industrialized and took on the status of a rising power, establishing
formal diplomatic relations with most European countries in the 1890s.

Roosevelt began to pay close attention to Japan in 1897 when he was assistant secretary of the navy. A few years earlier, President Harrison had tried to annex the Hawaiian Islands; the attempt failed when his successor in the White House, Grover Cleveland, abruptly returned the islands to the Hawaiians, an act that Roosevelt denounced as "a colossal crime" because it left the islands at the mercy of other foreign powers.[1]

With the largest navy in the world, Britain had the power to seize Hawaii for itself, but Roosevelt was more worried about Japan. He consequently urged President McKinley to send the battleship *Oregon* to Hawaii as a precautionary measure. He also directed the Naval War College to develop contingency plans for a Pacific war between the United States and Japan centered on Hawaii.[2] "I am fully alive to the danger of Japan," he told the hawkish strategist Alfred Thayer Mahan, bemoaning the fact that the American naval presence in the Pacific Ocean was practically non-existent.[3] To remedy this weakness, he wanted the United States to immediately annex Hawaii (Pearl Harbor would make a splendid base for the American fleet), build a canal through Central America to ensure the fast transit of U.S. warships from the Atlantic to Pacific oceans (it took more than two months for them to travel around South America), and build a dozen more battleships (four were currently afloat) so that a powerful fleet of sixteen battleships could protect American interests as a single fighting unit (he hated the idea of dividing the fleet).

After the United States annexed Hawaii as a U.S. Territory in 1898, Roosevelt's fear of an immediate confrontation with Japan over the islands faded, but his interest in Japan grew. He was drawn to the warlike culture of the Japanese, to their Samurai tradition of sword-bearing knights. While the Samurai were long gone, he saw that their martial spirit remained a driving force in the country. He worried it gave the Japanese a fighting edge over the United States, which he believed had grown soft and weak from the prosperity generated by the industrial revolution. The Boxer Rebellion in China confirmed his fears. He wrote to his friend Cecil Spring-Rice that the Japanese, who had fought with the European forces against the Boxers, had performed exceedingly well.

"What extraordinary soldiers the little Japs are! Our own troops out in China write, grudgingly, that they think the Japs did better than any of the allied forces. They put themselves and the English next."[4]

His admiration of the Japanese sprang in large part from his respect for their courage and prowess in battle, and also from the way they had suddenly stepped up to the top shelf of global powers. While worried this new Asiatic power threatened the United States, he was hopeful Japan, with its "strange alien civilization," would make "desirable additions" to the international society of nations.[5] It was in this hopeful spirit that he viewed the country throughout his presidency. In 1902, when both the British and Japanese governments informed him they were negotiating a new treaty of alliance and asked his views on the subject, he welcomed the news. Seeing the treaty would recognize Japan's place among the great powers, while also protecting the vital commercial interests of the United States in China by guaranteeing the so-called Open Door by which Western nations enjoyed equal commercial access to Chinese markets, he "entirely approved of the treaty."[6]

His hearty support for the Anglo-Japanese alliance might seem surprising to us given his fear in 1897 that Japan stood poised to seize Hawaii. But once the American flag flew over Pearl Harbor, the immediate danger from Japan was superseded by the growing threat from Russia, which held a vast amount of territory in Asia. Russia had promised to support the Open Door in China, but the United States and Britain had little faith in the pledge. By 1902, it was clear to both the American and British governments that Russia wanted to dominate the region at their expense. It had built up Vladivostok in Eastern Siberia for use as a military base and constructed the five-thousand-mile-long Trans-Siberian railroad to connect St. Petersburg and Moscow to distant Asia. It already had resource-rich Manchuria, and seemed poised to invade the rest of China, perhaps seeking to annex it and close the previously "Open Door" to British and American trade.

American expansion into the western Pacific after the Spanish-American War greatly increased the importance of the Open Door policy to the United States. In the words of the *Baltimore Sun*: "The

Hawaiian islands, Guam and the Philippines, with the command of the Pacific, are worthless to us if we cannot have access to the markets of the 400,000,000 people of the Chinese Empire, Manchuria included."[7] For many politicians, commerce was the primary rationale for an American empire. Senator Albert Beveridge of Indiana exclaimed: "Fate has written our policy for us. The trade of the world must and shall be ours. We shall establish trading posts throughout the world.... Our institutions will follow our flag on the wings of our commerce."[8]

America's tradition of avoiding "entangling alliances" with foreign nations meant Roosevelt could not make the United States a member of the Anglo-Japanese alliance, but as a British newspaper noted, he was "virtually a party [to the treaty] from the beginning" in his like-minded desire to maintain the territorial integrity of China and its openness to western trade.[9]

RUSSIA AND JAPAN GO TO WAR

As much as Roosevelt wanted to protect American interests in China, he had a larger concern when war between Russia and Japan suddenly erupted in 1903. A believer in the balance of power as the most effective means to maintain regional stability, he saw that a decisive victory by either side could be detrimental to the United States. If Russia won, it would increase the danger that American trade with China would be closed; if Japan won, it might mean something even worse. The Philippines and Hawaii would then be vulnerable to a hostile power "flushed with the glory of their recent triumph" over Russia and "bent upon establishing themselves as the leading power in the Pacific."[10] Ideally, Roosevelt wanted the Russo-Japanese War to end in a costly draw. He hoped both sides would "bleed themselves white" during a long war, explaining to a confidante: "If Japan and Russia, by heavy loss of men and treasure can be forced into long years of peace, it would be much better for every country having interests in the Pacific.... I would rather see the war go on until the two countries are utterly exhausted than stop it."[11]

Hoping for a long war between equally matched contestants, Roosevelt was disturbed to learn Germany and France were considering entering the conflict on Russia's side, just as they had in 1894 when the three had combined to force Japan to withdraw from Manchuria in humiliating fashion. He "notified Germany and France in the most polite and discreet fashion that in the event of a combination against Japan" the United States would "promptly side with Japan and proceed to whatever length was necessary on her behalf."[12] Knowing the British government "would act in the same way"[13] he did, he felt confident Germany and France would back down. In the end, they did. It was another example of Roosevelt's deep understanding of international politics.

As the war progressed, Japan performed remarkably well on the battlefield against the Russians. With Japan's decisive victory on land at Mukden in March 1905 and on the sea with the annihilation of the Russian fleet at Tsushima two months later, the war was virtually decided in Japan's favor even as the fighting continued. Disturbed by these dramatic events, TR ratcheted up his diplomatic efforts, urging the Russian government through its ambassador in Washington to immediately begin peace negotiations. Confiding in his close friend, the British diplomat Cecil Spring-Rice, he wrote in June 1905: "It may take six or eight months or a year if the war goes on, but in the end, at some such period of time, the Japs will have taken Vladivostok and Harbin and driven the Russians completely from the Pacific coast and eastern Asia."[14] Roosevelt tried and failed to convince the Russians to cut their losses. It was the victorious but financially strapped Japanese, who now occupied Manchuria and Korea, who decided that the war should end. The Japanese ambassador in Washington asked President Roosevelt to mediate a peace treaty between the warring powers. Roosevelt promptly accepted and agreed to present the peace initiative publicly as if it were his own idea, so that Japan could save face. Under intense diplomatic pressure from Germany, Russia finally agreed to meet Japan to discuss peace terms.

Russia's de facto defeat meant that Roosevelt's primary goal, the continuance of the Open Door policy in China, was a *fait accompli*. His secondary goal was to ensure a regional balance of power. Japan saw

Roosevelt as a sympathetic mediator and hoped he would help it claim a $600 million indemnity from Russia. But Roosevelt realized that it was Russia that now needed shoring up, not Japan.

Japan's demand was enormous: a budget of $600 million would have allowed the United States to build at least forty battleships (it had only sixteen afloat at the end of TR's presidency). The annual budget of the American government at the time was only around $700 million. If Japan had succeeded in squeezing Russia for the money, it would have dramatically shifted the balance of power in Asia. The last thing he wanted was a heightened Japanese military threat to the Philippines and Hawaii, so he put his full weight on the Russian side of the indemnity issue—the major bone of contention in the negotiation—and convinced Japan to withdraw its demand.

Roosevelt's brokering of the subsequent Treaty of Portsmouth, ending the Russo-Japanese War, won him international acclaim as a peacemaker. When he returned to Washington in October 1905, "hundreds of thousands of people lined Pennsylvania Avenue," waving hats and handkerchiefs as his horse-drawn carriage drove slowly up the avenue toward the White House. The *London Times* wondered if it was "the apogee of Mr. Roosevelt's career?"[15]

BETRAYING KOREA

In Japan, the public—which knew only of Japan's military and naval successes and not of the financial strains on the country—reacted to the treaty as if it had been a humiliating diplomatic defeat, and there were riots in Tokyo. But in fact the treaty was a major geopolitical victory for Japan—more so perhaps than Roosevelt intended—as the Japanese were recognized as the predominant power in Manchuria and Korea.

Critics contend, rightly, that the treaty failed to block Japan's imperial ambitions in their infancy, and, moreover, the effect of the treaty was to violate an 1883 treaty agreement between the United States and Korea in which both countries pledged to "exert their good offices" if other powers dealt "unjustly or oppressively with either government."[16] The Korean emperor invoked that clause after the Japanese took over Korea's government. Roosevelt, however, refused to oppose Japan, abruptly closed the United States legation in Korea, and recalled American diplomats from the country. In addition, Secretary of State Elihu Root turned away the entreaties of Homer Hulbert, an American citizen who served as Korea's special diplomatic representative to the United States.[17] But short of war—and the U.S. Navy had few ships in the Pacific Ocean in 1905—there was little Roosevelt could do to prevent Japan from seizing Korea, a point Elihu Root made twenty-five years later when he said: "Many people are still angry because we did not keep Japan from taking Korea. There was nothing we could do except fight Japan. Congress wouldn't have declared war and the people would have turned out the Congress that had. All we might have done was to make threats which we could not carry out."[18]

In Roosevelt's *realpolitik* sacrificing Korea was a small price to pay for maintaining Japanese-American relations, and thereby offering some diplomatic protection for the Philippines and Hawaii. Earlier, before he became president, he had even seen a Japanese occupation of Korea as a positive outcome: "I should like to see Japan have Korea," he told a German diplomat in 1900. "She will be a check upon Russia, and she deserves it for what she has done. But I do earnestly hope there will be no slicing up of China. It will be bad for everybody in the end."[19]

In the summer of 1905, prior to the opening of peace negotiations at Portsmouth, TR had sent William Howard Taft to Japan as a special emissary to take the temperature of its government. After his discussion Taft cabled a "memorandum of conversation" back to TR in Washington in which he described Japan's desire that the United States acquiesce in its domination of Korea in return for an assurance that it would not menace Hawaii or the Philippines. Taft assured Japanese leaders that TR would agree to this arrangement, and he was right; TR quickly cabled back: "Your conversation with Count Katsura absolutely correct in every respect. Wish you could state to Katsura that I confirm every word you have said."[20]

If TR felt any guilt over Korea, perhaps he rationalized that Japanese colonial rule would lift the backward Koreans into modernity, just as other imperial powers, including the United States, told themselves they were taking on the "white man's burden" to help lesser developed peoples. But Roosevelt, as well read as he was, should have realized that such a sense of *noblesse oblige* was a product of the Christian West and did not carry into the alien civilization of Japan, which cared little for the human rights of individuals according to Western norms. TR had read books that described Japan's warlike character, listened to eyewitness accounts of the brutal conduct of Japanese soldiers during the Russo-Japanese War, and admitted a military conflict against Japan would mean "rapine on their part, not war."[21] Yet he had no qualms about warlike Japan ruling the peaceful Koreans. Perhaps he thought it was inevitable.

It is easy, especially given Japan's barbaric behavior during its decades-long occupation of Korea (it only ended after Japan's defeat in 1945), to criticize Roosevelt for abandoning the Hermit Kingdom. In return for ignoring an American treaty obligation to Korea, he gained a Japanese promise that it would not threaten the Philippines and Hawaii, a promise that proved reliable for over thirty years, a major achievement in helping to protect American interests in the Pacific.[22] The Japanese respected Roosevelt, some hated him (he was "cartooned as an enemy of Japan"[23] during the Tokyo riots), but his sacrifice of Korea to safeguard the Philippines and Hawaii, gave them the impression that he feared Japanese power. Sensing weakness in the American president, the Japanese government decided to take a more forceful approach in dealing with the United States after California began to pass discriminatory laws against Japanese migrants.

JAPANESE IMMIGRATION CONTROVERSY

The influx of "coolies" from Asia had long been a contentious issue on the Pacific Coast, prompting labor groups to sporadically erupt in fury at the foreign laborers who undercut the wages of American citizens and took their jobs. The Chinese Exclusion law, first enacted in 1882 (signed by President Arthur after he threatened a veto, then extended ten years later by the Geary Act, and made "permanent" until it was repealed in the 1940s), barred Chinese laborers from entering the country but did nothing about Japanese immigrants. There were only about ten thousand of these in California, yet their presence nonetheless became a lightning rod for labor agitation and the state government tried to enact laws to bar their entrance into the state. Fearful California might provoke a war with Japan by enacting discriminatory legislation, Roosevelt vented his frustration to Henry Cabot Lodge in June 1905:

> These Pacific coast people wish grossly to insult the Japanese and to keep out the Japanese immigrants on the ground that they are an immoral, degraded and worthless race, and at the same time...they expect to be given advantages in Oriental markets, and with besotted folly are indifferent to building up the navy while provoking this formidable new power—a power jealous, sensitive and warlike, and which if irritated could at once take both the Philippines and Hawaii from us if she obtained the upper hand on the seas.[24]

The immigrant controversy intensified after a massive earthquake struck San Francisco in April 1906, destroying many of the city's schools. Unable to accommodate all students in the buildings that remained standing, the San Francisco School Board decided to bar Japanese children from attending school. As blacks were segregated from whites throughout the South and Chinese laborers were barred from entering the country altogether, discrimination against the Japanese was nothing out of the ordinary. The Japanese in California, however, had a powerful friend in the "jealous, sensitive and warlike" nation from which they hailed on the other side of the Pacific Ocean—a nation eager to use any issue it could to gain the upper hand on the United States. And like clockwork, immediately after the San Francisco School Board announced its decision, Japan's ambassador to the United States visited Secretary of State Elihu Root and delivered a strong protest, telling him that discrimination against Japanese children by the United States was "resented very bitterly by all Japanese."[25]

In a time when most Americans accepted racial discrimination, the Japanese ambassador's protest lacked the moral authority it would have commanded today. But it was backed by the 1894 treaty of friendship between the United States and Japan, which gave the children of Japanese immigrants the right to attend public schools. The ambassador told Root his government expected the Roosevelt administration to honor the existing treaty, and give the Japanese in California their full rights and privileges under its terms. A compromise was soon reached between the two countries: Japan agreed to voluntarily limit the migration of its people to the United States; the American government, in turn, agreed to rein in the state of California.

This gentleman's agreement defused the crisis for a while, but in May 1907, a labor riot in San Francisco directed against the Japanese spiked tensions again. Commenting on the incident the *Nichi Nichi*, a Tokyo newspaper, struck an ominous editorial that seemed like a threat to the United States:

> Even traditional friendship will not escape a rupture should incidents like those that have occurred in San Francisco be repeated.... What we want are not so many expressions of civilized sentiments, but one act of efficient protection for the treaty rights of the Japanese. The waste paper box is no destination for a treaty between Japan and the United States.[26]

PUTTING JAPAN ON NOTICE: THE GREAT WHITE FLEET

Hearing the war drums from across the Pacific Ocean, Roosevelt grew increasingly uneasy. His fears were exacerbated when the British and German governments warned him war was certain unless conditions changed radically.[27] He had taken extraordinary steps to placate Japan by strong-arming California, but now began to think his efforts to resolve the controversy with peaceful diplomacy had backfired, causing Japan to see him as a weak leader afraid of Asia's newest power. Deciding he needed to refute this notion, he ordered the massive U.S. fleet, including all sixteen battleships then afloat, into the Pacific Ocean on a "training cruise."

No doubt, he sincerely wanted to increase the efficiency of the U.S. Navy by sending it on a long voyage. But his principle goal was to put Japan on notice that he would not be bullied and that the U.S. fleet was a stronger foe than the Russian fleet Japan had annihilated at Tsushima in 1905. In April 1908, after the battle fleet had embarked on its journey to the Pacific Ocean, Roosevelt explained his reasoning to his military aide Archie Butt:

> I sent it around the world because I wanted to give Tokyo an object lesson. The fleet is our first line of defense. In case of a war with Japan it would prove our salvation. If the Japanese could sink it, as they did the Russian fleet at Port Arthur, they could land a quarter of a million men on our Pacific Coast and it would take us several years and cost us an enormous sum in men and money to dislodge them. The Japs have been very cocky since the war with Russia, but they will hesitate to molest us as long as we carry a big stick.... The Japanese leaders and Court have lost much prestige by what they think was their failure to crush Russia, and while the terms they secured at Portsmouth were much more than they could have secured six months later, the treaty was not altogether satisfactory to the nation and sooner or later they will try to bolster up their power by another war. Unfortunately for us we have what they want most, the Philippines.[28]

Roosevelt did not understate the threat. As Graf von Reventlow, editor-in-chief of Germany's *Army and Navy Journal*, observed in 1907: "The Japanese can make themselves masters of the Philippine Islands any day with perfect ease and at a minimum cost."[29]

Consequently, the voyage of the Great White Fleet was a strategic triumph. Circumventing the globe in 1908, the twenty-six-ship armada announced to the world that the United States was a power that could not be ignored. Stopping along the way in Japan, it reinforced the message that an attack on the Philippines and Hawaii would be resisted by a naval force second only to Britain's. While Japan issued no protests and showed "absolute sang-froid over the massing of the American warships in the Pacific,"[30] its aggressive diplomatic assault against the United States suddenly ceased. It is impossible to know for sure, but the dramatic voyage of the "battle fleet" (as Roosevelt insisted on calling it) in all likelihood prevented war.

CHAPTER EIGHTEEN

PANAMA: MAKING THE DIRT FLY

~

T he greatest engineering feat of its age, the Panama Canal, remains one of the man-made wonders of the world. It opened in 1914 thanks to Theodore Roosevelt who, a decade earlier, had used "Gunboat Diplomacy" to secure the narrow strip of land upon which the canal was eventually built.

Most Americans appeared to support TR's strong-arm methods used to acquire the land. But many liberal-minded observers, concerned with abstract notions of international justice, condemned his precipitate action. Ignoring his legion of liberal critics, TR glowed with pride over his achievement, boasting "the building of the canal through Panama will rank in kind, though not of course in degree, with the Louisiana Purchase and the acquisition of Texas."[1]

Roosevelt's administration negotiated a treaty that purchased America sovereignty over the Canal Zone "in perpetuity"; and TR, the man who "made the dirt fly," would almost certainly have regarded President Jimmy Carter's transfer of the Canal Zone to Panamanian sovereignty

as a sign of weakness, like so many other foreign policy decisions of the
Carter administration. Roosevelt had no qualms about American imperialism, seeing it as an engine of progress. Liberals, like Carter, on the
other hand, have regarded it as unjust if not illegal. Ronald Reagan, who
defeated Carter in the next presidential election, took TR's side, but did
not try to undo Carter's action.

THE GREAT PROJECT

The idea of building a canal through Central America to enable ships
to move quickly between the Atlantic and Pacific oceans was first con-
ceived in the late 1500s. It took another three hundred years before a
concrete plan to build a canal got off the ground. In 1879, the renowned
French engineer, Ferdinand de Lesseps, formed the Panama Canal Company with the goal of constructing a man-made waterway through the
isthmus of Panama. Soon thereafter, the company won a concession from
Colombia (which owned the isthmus), allowing the company to proceed
with the ambitious project. During the next decade the project devolved
into a gigantic Ponzi scheme and went bankrupt in 1889. The investigation that followed revealed the company had squandered $70 million of
the $156 million raised to build the canal.

The United States had long wanted a canal through Central America.
The U.S. Navy's experience in the Spanish-American War—when it took
more than two months for the battleship *Oregon* to steam around Cape
Horn to fight the Spanish fleet off Cuba—gave new impetus to the desire;
it became a national-security necessity. Many preferred a route through
Nicaragua; others through the isthmus of Panama. In 1902, the U.S.
government bought the Panama Canal Company for $40 million, includ-
ing its concession from Colombia.

Believing a Panama canal could be finished in less time than the
Nicaraguan alternative, President Roosevelt offered Colombia $10 mil-
lion for a ten-mile wide strip of the Panamanian Isthmus. The U.S. Senate ratified the proposed treaty in March 1903, but a strong opposition
movement in Colombia's legislature foiled the deal.

By September 1903, Roosevelt had three alternatives. He could open a new round of negotiations with Colombia's government (it now wanted $20 million for the territory, which TR believed was evidence that delays and demands for bribes would continue *ad infinitum*). He could proceed under the Spooner Act of 1902, which gave him the option of negotiating with Nicaragua. Or he could "allow matters to drift."[2] He chose the third option—but with a purpose.

ROOSEVELT BULLIES HIS WAY

Roosevelt told Rudyard Kipling that he would never again do business with Colombia, "a corrupt pithecoid community in which the President has obtained his position by the simple process of clapping the former President into a wooden cage and sending him on an ox cart over the mountains—this is literally what was done at Bogota."[3] The United States had granted diplomatic recognition to Colombia in 1822, during James Monroe's administration, but Roosevelt told Kipling it was preposterous to believe Colombia was "entitled to just the treatment that I would give, say, to Denmark or Switzerland."[4] To him the government of Colombia was entitled to no more respect than "a group of Sicilian or Calabrian banditry."[5]

Roosevelt's inaction had its reasons. He thought—as many foreign policy analysts did—that the Panamanians would revolt if Colombia rejected the treaty. While some believe TR inspired the uprising in Panama—a charge he always denied ("I did not foment the revolution on the Isthmus")[6]—he simply believed it was inevitable.

As early as June—a full five months before the revolution began—the *Baltimore Sun* prophesized: "If Colombia refuses to ratify the treaty it is believed the two provinces of Panama and Cauca will take the matter into their own hands, and, with the moral support of the United States, secede from the sovereignty of Colombia."[7] TR had talked with two U.S. military officers who had been in Panama and with William Nelson Cromwell (the general counsel of the new Panama Canal Company) to gather intelligence; acting on all he learned, he decided to order U.S. naval vessels to the isthmus in case they were needed.

His order came too late to place a full complement of American war-ships in the area when the long-anticipated uprising broke out on Novem-ber 3, 1903. The revolution was nearly bloodless (one Chinaman was killed when a Colombian warship shelled Panama City). Colombia had only five hundred troops in Panama. They quickly surrendered to the rebels, and Roosevelt informed the Colombian government he would not permit the landing of any more Colombian troops on the isthmus. He explained that under the U.S. Treaty of 1846 with New Grenada (the former name of Colombia) his duty was to ensure safe transit across the isthmus. The U.S. Navy, therefore, would not allow a civil war in the territory. After ten American warships arrived at the isthmus—five on the Pacific Ocean side, five on the Caribbean Sea side—Panama's independence was virtually guaranteed, as forbidding mountains and impenetrable swamps provided natural, land-based barriers to a Colombian invasion.

While Roosevelt was right that he had a treaty obligation to protect American interests in Panama and to keep its commercial corridor open, he conveniently forgot that the very same treaty also stated that the United States guaranteed "the rights of sovereignty and property which New Grenada (Colombia) has and possesses over the same territory."[8] In doing so, he brazenly overrode the precedent established in 1885 by President Grover Cleveland, who sent warships to Panama and landed U.S. Marines on the isthmus when a rebellion erupted, but did not inter-fere when Colombia used force to put down the uprising.

Recognizing that significant U.S. national interests were now at stake, TR seized his opportunity and officially recognized the indepen-dence of the new Republic of Panama on November 7, 1903—only four days after the revolution began. A month later, Panama accepted an amended version of the canal treaty that Colombia had rejected. In TR's defense, it is important to note significant worries that hung over his head as he acted. He feared, and for good reason, losing what might be his one chance to acquire the Canal Zone for the United States. He recalled how President Benjamin Harrison's attempt to annex Hawaii in 1892 had been reversed by his successor in the White House, Grover Cleveland, because Congress had not decided the matter by the time

Harrison left office. TR realized the same thing could happen to him if he did not act quickly and get Congress's stamp of approval. The 1904 presidential election was only a year away and his victory was not guaranteed. By comparison, Cleveland's intervention in 1885 did not involve the canal issue, making it much easier to resolve.

THE MIXED VERDICT

While Roosevelt's action was popular at home—where it was seen as a boon to American commerce and as the liberation of a subject people (the Panamanians)—the reaction of foreign nations was mixed, welcoming the potential benefits to trade, but also assuming that the United States had cooked up the Panamanian revolution in order to steal the isthmus from Colombia. In Britain, the *London Times* captured the prevailing view when it declared "the President's masterful hand is visible in all" that had gone on in Panama,[9] an opinion echoed by the German newspaper *Vossische Zeitung*, which declared: "The reason why the President waited two months after Colombia rejected the treaty without negotiating with Nicaragua is now clear—the United States was finding an effective way of attaining its ends by working behind the scenes."[10]

Meanwhile, indignation swept across Latin America, with a Mexican newspaper denouncing the "Saxon perfidy" of the United States in engineering a "farcical" revolution to achieve "the dismemberment of the unhappy Colombia."[11] Some members of the U.S. press were equally critical. Horrified at Roosevelt's brazen imperialism, the liberal-minded *New York Times* branded the administration's action "a national disgrace,"[12] declaring the "transaction put a stain upon our name, a blot upon our reputation for international fair dealing won by a century of honorable neutrality."[13] When Roosevelt asked his Secretary of War Elihu Root what he thought, Root, a Wall Street lawyer, responded: "You have shown that you were accused of seduction and you have conclusively proved that you were guilty of rape."[14] One has to assume this is not the endorsement TR sought.

SOWING LATIN AMERICAN DISCONTENT

While Roosevelt's brute force broke the diplomatic logjam that had prevented construction of the canal, it created other diplomatic problems. Latin American governments, for instance, at the 1907 Hague Conference opposed U.S. proposals for a permanent court of justice, assuming it would be skewed in the interests of the great powers.

According to the *New York Times*, the Latin American representatives "accused the United States of having neglected them and of caring only for working in accord with Great Britain and Germany, thinking that a union with these great powers would be sufficient to carry out any project...."[15]

Roosevelt believed, rightly, that the Panama Canal was a monumental achievement that was of immense benefit to the United States and the world. (In its first hundred years, more than a million ships passed through Panama Canal.) In 1914, he was infuriated to learn that the Wilson administration had negotiated a new treaty with Colombia. Under its terms, the United States would pay Colombia a $25 million indemnity for the loss of Panama and officially apologize for misconduct in acquiring the Panama Canal Zone. Roosevelt fired off a letter of protest to the chairman of the Senate Foreign Relations Committee and asked to testify to defend his actions with regard to Panama. He denounced the proposed treaty as "a crime against the United States" and declared his actions in securing the Canal Zone were taken "in accordance with the highest principles of international, of national, and of private morality."[16]

Roosevelt's Republican allies in the Senate blocked ratification of the proposed treaty until after TR's death.

In 1921, Republican President Warren Harding revived discussion of the treaty. After redacting the apology to Colombia, Harding won strong support for it among Senate Republicans. Even Roosevelt's old friend, Senator Henry Cabot Lodge, voted for it, helping it pass by a 69-to-19 margin. That very fact showed a guilty American conscience, and regret for the hard feelings Roosevelt's precipitate action had caused in Latin America, and also that new national interests were now at stake (American oil companies wanted to win oil concessions in Colombia). But whatever the diplomatic fallout, and it was considerable and lasting, the canal stands as his monument, an undeniable achievement of the first order.

CHAPTER NINETEEN

MONROE DOCTRINE: ADDING A POLICE POWER

~

Theodore Roosevelt's second blow to cordial diplomatic relations between the United States and Latin America occurred when he declared his "Roosevelt Corollary" to the Monroe Doctrine. The United States reserved the right, he said, to intervene in the affairs of Latin American states that "misbehaved." The United States would now be, as the *New York Evening Post* put it, "the Big Policeman" of the Western Hemisphere.[1] Under today's notions of international law, such aggressive assertions of national power are denied by the Western world, with the United States and its allies denouncing Vladimir Putin's interventions in Crimea and Ukraine under Russia's version of the Monroe Doctrine.

Roosevelt believed that his public expansion of the Monroe Doctrine would help the United States avoid a replay of the Venezuelan Crisis of 1902, and prevent future European military incursions into the Western Hemisphere. He was actually trying to undo the rhetorical blunder he made in his First Annual Message to Congress in 1901 when he announced the United States would not allow the Monroe Doctrine to shield any Latin American nation "against punishment [from European powers] if it misconducts itself provided that punishment does not take the form of the acquisition of territory by any non-American power."[2] He compounded that error when he told the German Ambassador Speck von Sternberg: "If any South American country misbehaves toward any European country, let the European country spank it."[3] The word *spank* highlighted like nothing else his paternalistic belief that the Latin peoples who lived south of the Rio Grande were wayward children who needed periodic correction.

Roosevelt told Cecil Spring-Rice that "each part of the world should be prosperous and well policed."[4] In the Western Hemisphere that was the job of the United States. The Roosevelt Corollary was put into action in 1904, during the Santo Domingo Crisis.

Santo Domingo (today called the Dominican Republic) was in perpetual turmoil and the United States had already intervened on the island in February 1904 when Roosevelt ordered a small punitive expedition against Dominican rebels who had killed an American seaman and attacked American property on the island. Looming over the seemingly endless crises in Santo Domingo, where it was quipped that the governing model was "tyranny tempered by assassination," was that the government had ceased debt payments to its European creditors. Fearful that another Venezuelan crisis might materialize, Roosevelt said in March 1904: "I want to do nothing but what a policeman has to do in San Domingo."

In January 1905 the Roosevelt administration announced that it had negotiated an agreement with the Santo Domingo government. The United States would protect the island's territorial integrity—shielding it from European intervention—and take over its customs houses, using a percentage of the proceeds to pay off the government's foreign creditors. (The revenue generated by Santo Domingo's tariff duties was redirected into New York banks, with the accumulated money under the management of an American commission appointed by the president; this fund was used to service San Domingo's outstanding debt obligations to Europe.) The U.S. Senate was appalled that TR had taken this action on his own, but Elihu Root painstakingly revised the agreement into a treaty that was approved by the Senate in February 1907.

TR's action assuming control of the Customs House was the first use of "Dollar Diplomacy." "'Dollar Diplomacy' implied an American financial protectorate, or something approaching a financial protectorate, over bankrupt Caribbean states," wrote the *London Times*. "San Domingo is the first," it added, "and so far the sole example of its operation,"[5] though following TR's precedent, the Taft administration set up more such financial protectorates, where the United States took responsibility for shoring up economic and political stability in countries with American financial interests, including Honduras and Nicaragua, in part, it was said, to protect America's strategic position over the Panama Canal.

Roosevelt, in announcing his corollary, had stated that any Latin American nation that conducted itself well, "acting with decency in industrial and political matters, keeping order, and paying its obligations" need not fear interference. The United States would only intervene when there was "brutal wrongdoing or impotence which results in the general loosening of the ties of civilized society."[6]

Britain (which managed its vast empire using a similar approach, as for example in Egypt, where it intervened to protect the Suez Canal despite the fact that the Ottoman Empire still was nominally the sovereign power in that territory) and the rest of Europe (which took colonialism in stride) had few criticisms of Roosevelt. Elsewhere, critics howled at the overbearing tone of Roosevelt's Corollary to the Monroe Doctrine. The *New York Sun* was astounded at the president's "language of menace," pointing out there was no nation in Latin America "with whom this republic is not on terms of friendship, treaty, amity, perfect peace and good will."[7]

The Roosevelt Corollary did, in fact, deny European nations a financial pretext for intervening in Latin American states. But critics believed it was also entirely unnecessary. Richard Olney, for instance, who had been Secretary of State under President Grover Cleveland, and who had vigorously defended the Monroe Doctrine in 1895 during the border dispute between Venezuela and Britain, thought the new policy was ill-advised, writing: "Our institutions will surely live and our people continue to prosper without the United States converting itself into an international policeman for the American continents or into a debt-collecting agency for the benefit of foreign creditor states and their citizens."[8]

PLAYING NICE WITH CUBA

Cuba was a bright spot in Roosevelt's Latin American policy. A movement existed during his presidency to annex the island. Despite his reputation as the "Imperialist of Imperialists,"[9] TR refused to go along with the idea. Prior to the Spanish-American War, the United States had declared through the Teller Amendment it had no intention of permanently acquiring Cuba. After Spain was defeated in 1898, the island became a temporary American possession. In 1902, Roosevelt recognized Cuba as an independent state.

By granting Cuba its independence, Roosevelt proved he was no insatiable imperialist, and also that he was a prudent politician. If he had pushed for annexation, he would have been opposed by anti-imperialist liberals; by politicians who thought the Cubans were not ready for self-government on the U.S. model (TR himself was actually in this camp); by the Sugar Trust (one of the most powerful monopolies at the time), which feared cheap Cuban sugar (no longer inflated by tariff duties) would undercut their prices and their profits; and by Democrat-dominated Southern states, which before the Civil War had been ardent for annexing Cuba as a slave state, but which now saw it as a state with a largely black population that would be in the pocket of the Republicans. Roosevelt knew that Cuban independence in no way threatened American interests, because the United States retained the right to intervene if necessary on the island, and to lease land for a naval base (which became the American naval base at Guantanamo Bay).

Roosevelt sincerely wanted Cuba to succeed as an independent nation, and to that end he persuaded Congress, against stiff opposition, to lower duties on Cuban imports. When rebellion rocked the young Cuban Republic in August 1906, after the allegedly fraudulent election of President Tomas Estrada Palma, TR intervened by sending his secretary of war, William Howard Taft, along with U.S. warships, to Cuba, to tell Palma that he must agree to a new election to legitimize his authority. Palma refused and abruptly resigned his office, and Taft became provisional governor of the island. About a thousand U.S. Marines were landed to protect American interests, but they were not needed as Palma's resignation calmed the political opposition, who put down their arms to await a new election.

Once a new Cuban government was elected, the United States promptly handed over the reins of power and removed its troops and ships from the area. Roosevelt's statesmanship in quickly resolving the crisis deserves praise; his actions were both restrained and forceful. He had hoped to avoid an armed intervention by convincing President Palma to hold a new election. When that failed, TR reluctantly saw he had to take temporary control of the island. In helping Cuba to avoid a bloody civil war, he again resisted those who wanted to bring the island into the United States, declaring: "Cuba must have another chance. Annexation is not to be thought of in this moment. We must regard the republic as a car which has been overturned, and we must put our shoulders to the side, restore it to its wheels, and start it off again under the control of a competent engineer."[10]

For Roosevelt, American leadership could make the world a better place, and an American cop on the beat of the western hemisphere not only secured American interests but gave the nations of Latin America their best chance for stability and prosperity.

PART V

ASSESSING

HIS TWO

TERMS

~

CHAPTER TWENTY

ONE OF THE GREATEST PRESIDENTS

~

A ny assessment of Theodore Roosevelt's presidency would look, of course, at his domestic and foreign policies. But it would also have to look at how Roosevelt reinvigorated American democracy. In that role, he earns an "A+." In the generation that preceded him, wealthy special interests and corrupt political machines largely determined the outcome of elections. This corrupt, dysfunctional political system did not disappear overnight, but TR forced it to the margins by making a direct appeal to the American people from his bully pulpit in the White House. This was arguably his greatest achievement as president.

Libertarians still criticize Theodore Roosevelt for expanding government at the beginning of the twentieth century, but they measure Roosevelt's actions by where America is today, not where America was when Roosevelt was president; different times require different reforms. Historian William Harbaugh wrote in 1961: "Theodore Roosevelt's greatest contribution to American life, historians now agree, was the awakening of the people to the need for even further reform."[1] But it is to TR's credit that such reform was tempered by conservative principles of fiscal prudence, a preference for a free, competitive economy, and a robust defense of traditional moral values. TR's enemy was socialism, and his reforms prevented socialism from getting a foothold in the United States.

That point is often neglected. More obvious is that Roosevelt helped transform America into a world power in the twentieth century. No country could in future ignore the economic, diplomatic, and potential military power of the United States, which, whatever TR's belligerent reputation, was used to advance the cause of international peace. No previous American president had the international stature of Theodore Roosevelt; and never had the United States been so highly respected in global affairs.

GRADING HIS DOMESTIC POLICY

Roosevelt's domestic policy achievements may look paltry in comparison to those of his progressive successor in the White House, Woodrow Wilson, but judged by their own merits they were outstanding and deserve nothing less than an "A" grade.

Overall Grade	A
Conservation	A+
Reclamation/Irrigation	A+
Settling the Anthracite Coal Strike	A
Pure Food and Meat Inspection Laws	A
Anti-Trust Policy	B-
Sidestepping the Tariff	B-
Race Relations	C+
Currency/Banking Reform	D-

Conservation of the nation's natural resources and reclamation of the arid lands of the West stand out as the sparkling gems of Roosevelt's

domestic record. In the first case, he took a small movement of naturalists, hunters, and outdoorsmen, and turned it into a national movement
for preserving forests and wildlife that might have been lost without his
leadership; and he did so with an eye on making human use of renewable
resources. In the second case, he has never received the credit he deserves
for the creation of a gigantic water supply infrastructure that eventually
included, in the decades that followed his presidency, the construction
of seven hundred dams, which stand testimony to his vision of an American west opened up to irrigation and civilization.

He earns an "A" for the manner in which he resolved the Anthracite
Coal Strike that threatened to destabilize America's economy during the
winter of 1902–1903. Acting as no president had before, he skillfully
brought the antagonists together and forced a settlement by threatening
to use the U.S. Army to seize and operate the coal mines, explaining later
that the interests of the American people were paramount in the controversy. Future presidents used the precedent he set to justify similar interventions in labor disputes. He also earns an "A" for creating a new
regulatory regime to protect consumers from the danger of tainted meat
and from patent medicines that did not label their ingredients. These
Meat Inspection and Pure Food laws he championed laid the foundation
for the Food and Drug Administration, which continues to protect consumers today.

Roosevelt deserves praise for giving teeth to the Sherman anti-trust
law, which had been on the books for more than a decade when he
became president but was never enforced in a meaningful way. His
decision to blow the dust off of this neglected statute ultimately led to
the elimination of monopolistic corporations in the American economy
in the decades that followed—an achievement that was a huge benefit
to the United States; it ensured robust competition within the country's
free market system. By the end of his administration, however, his anti-
trust policy became so watered down that critics wondered whether he
had ever been sincere in trying to restrain the excesses of monopolistic
corporations. To some of his critics, especially later, it appeared that
the "trust buster" was actually more comfortable with big business

dominating the economy than he let on, and that he was tempted by the apparent rationality of a top-down industrial policy, such as was followed by Germany and Japan. For this reason, we give his anti-trust record a "B-" grade.

Roosevelt's refusal to tear down the high tariff wall, a wall that kept consumer prices artificially high and that, free market economists would argue, restrained economic growth, would seem to be one of the failures of his administration, yet we give him a "B-" because he almost certainly would have failed had he made the attempt to solve the problem. Seeing the certainty of a disastrous political defeat, he wisely focused on those things he could achieve. Wilson's success in lowering the tariff makes Roosevelt's record look weak in this respect; but it should be remembered that Wilson had the strong support of his party and the recent passage of the Sixteenth Amendment permitting the income tax, both of which made his task easier. It should also be pointed out that in both his moderation of his trust-busting and his avoidance of tariff reform, Roosevelt positioned himself with the more conservative elements of the Republican Party, which makes the claim that he was a "liberal progressive" even more absurd.

Roosevelt has received high praise for the example he set by inviting Booker T. Washington to dinner at the White House, but this symbolic gesture was not reflected in public policy. He did not have the power to end segregation in the South or reverse Supreme Court decisions that effectively muted the Fourteenth and Fifteenth Amendments, yet he could have mounted his bully pulpit to denounce segregation as a wicked and unjust system that needed to be abolished. That he did not speaks to his prudence as a politician. As with the tariff, he saw no point in entering a public policy battle he could not win.

His decision to discharge a regiment of black soldiers "without honor" from the U.S. Army after a shooting incident in Brownsville, Texas, was a terrible injustice in itself and also, because of the negative public reaction to it, a political mistake that cost the Republican Party some of its support among black voters. Moreover, his refusal to sit black delegates from the South at the Bull Moose Party convention in 1912 seems inexcusable in its needless pandering to potential white voters in the South who were overwhelmingly Democrats. For these reasons, we give his overall race record a "C+."

Inattention to currency and banking reform was the gaping hole in Roosevelt's presidency. He could have leveraged the Panic of 1907 to modernize the country's antiquated financial system. He took a pass instead, leaving the task to Woodrow Wilson, who set up the first central bank in the United States since Andrew Jackson destroyed its predecessor eighty years before. Frank Vanderlip, a leading light on Wall Street and later one of the architects of the Federal Reserve system, blamed TR's naïveté regarding economics and finance for the inaction, lamenting after the 1907 panic, "Mr. Roosevelt made speeches and issued Messages which added to the economic crisis—a crisis in confidence," adding:

> Mr. Roosevelt is not a financier. He is a preacher. He is not acquainted with questions of credit, of speculation. He chose the moment when those questions were the most delicate to occupy himself with them in a demonstrative way. He ought to have surrounded himself with specialists, to have taken their opinion, to have had conferences with them. But a conference with Mr. Roosevelt is almost always Mr. Roosevelt's conference. He talks too much, and is too lavish with epithets. Mind, I absolutely approve of his principles and moral views. All I say is that his method and manner have been bad. Before giving a patient a lesson in morals, the doctor has a first duty—namely, to cure him. Mr. Roosevelt neglected that common sense truth.[2]

It is ironic that critics of the Federal Reserve Board are also often critics of Theodore Roosevelt, but this reform—which they regard as "statist"—is one that he opposed.

The rest of Roosevelt's domestic record is otherwise impressive. He cleaned up corruption in the Post Office; pushed an employers' liability law through Congress that paved the way for the workmen's compensation laws that protect Americans who are injured on the job; streamlined the organization of the army and navy; secured statehood for Oklahoma; improved the management of the nation's inland waterways as part of his conservation and reclamation policies. On the negative side: he extended the discriminatory law that excluded Chinese immigrants from entering the United States and used his Justice Department to sue the newspaper mogul Joseph Pulitzer for libel—after becoming incensed at what he regarded as the "scurrilous" mendacity of the *New York World* newspaper, which he thought was libeling the good name of his administration and the United States government—a move that would have had a devastating impact on the freedom of the press had a wise judge not dismissed the suit as an unconstitutional violation of the First Amendment. On the whole, the good outweighs the bad, bolstering his overall grade in the domestic sphere to an "A."

GRADING HIS FOREIGN POLICY

Roosevelt was a master diplomat, a practitioner of *realpolitik*, and a passionate and intelligent advocate for America's national interests. His fault, especially in Latin America, was that he could at times appear overbearing and occasionally, as with Korea, dismissive of the rights of small nations.

Overall Grade	B
Peacekeeping and Peacemaking	A+
Leading the United States onto the World Stage	A+
Britain: Building Anglo-American "Special Relationship"	A
Germany: Restraining the Kaiser	A
Japan: Preventing War in the Pacific	B
Panama Canal: Making the Dirt Fly	C+
"Roosevelt Corollary" to Monroe Doctrine	D

The adroit manner in which Roosevelt protected and advanced American interests around the world while keeping the country at peace represents one of his most important achievements in the White House. On an individual level, he saw war as a noble endeavor that elevated the character of those who demonstrated courage under fire, but as a statesman he made extraordinary efforts to avoid it for his country's sake. Represented as a Napoleon on horseback during his administration, he left office with a record for peacekeeping and peacemaking that remains unmatched by any other president in American history. For this remarkable accomplishment, we give him an "A+."

That Roosevelt was a transcendent president in foreign policy is shown by the encomium he received from the *Washington Post* when he left the White House in 1909:

> In world politics he has written his name upon international history in a way no other President either attempted or succeeded in doing. He has introduced the United States to the assembly of nations as a power whose influence reaches not over the continent of the Americas where Monroe extended it, but over and around the world.[3]

In bilateral relations, Roosevelt's most underrated foreign policy achievement was ushering in a new era of Anglo-American friendship. Most people believe the "Special Relationship" between the United States and Britain was forged by Winston Churchill and Franklin Roosevelt during World War II. But the warming of ties between the two English-speaking peoples began in earnest during TR's administration. He used an extensive network of friends and acquaintances among Britain's governing class to cement the bond between the two nations.

Roosevelt also earns an "A" for the way in which he restrained the saber-rattling, unpredictable Kaiser Wilhelm II of Germany. Roosevelt not only deterred the kaiser from carving a new colony out of South America, but built a strong, personal diplomatic relationship with him that allowed Roosevelt to successfully mediate the Moroccan dispute in 1906. Roosevelt's policy toward Japan is less impressive. On the positive side, he sent the Great White Fleet around the world, an action that, with its message of American strength, helped prevent a major war in the Pacific for more than thirty years. He also shrewdly helped Russia while acting as mediator in the peace conference that ended the Russo-Japanese War, realizing a strong Russia in the Far East was in America's interest; it provided a needed offset to Japan's growing power. On the negative side, his policy of accommodation toward Japan, of allowing the island nation to do as it wanted within its "sphere of influence," helped create conditions in Asia that undoubtedly encouraged Japan's imperial ambitions. Specifically, his decision to look the other way as Japan annexed and brutalized Korea, despite a treaty obligation that made it the duty of the United States to use its "good offices" to help Korea against a foreign aggressor, is a stain on his foreign policy record.

Usually farsighted, Roosevelt failed to see that an American foreign policy that trampled on the dignity of weaker nations could have a long-term downside. The Panama Canal remains today one of the top engineering feats in world history and was in some respects a marvelous achievement of Roosevelt's foreign policy. Yet the manner in which it was achieved—ignoring a U.S. treaty obligation to guarantee Colombia's sovereignty over Panama and using American warships to protect the new Panamanian nation—and Roosevelt's declaration of his Corollary to the Monroe Doctrine angered many Latin American leaders, creating resentment against "Yankee imperialism" that exists to this day.

Granted, perhaps that resentment might have existed anyway, given the United States' predominance in the hemisphere; and granted that Roosevelt viewed his corollary as giving the United States a positive power to assist countries, to help them put their affairs in order. Nevertheless, when Franklin Roosevelt repudiated the corollary in the 1930s with his "Good Neighbor" policy, most Latin American leaders considered it a positive step.

TR's dealings with the rest of the world were largely positive, especially the skillful and largely benevolent way he governed the nation's new colonial empire. Contradicting his reputation as an insatiable expansionist intent on gobbling up territory around the world, he hauled down the American flag flying over Cuba and gave the island independence, fulfilling the promise the United States had made when it declared war on Spain. Not stopping there, he persuaded Congress to allow Cuban sugar to come into the United States without import duties to boost the island's weak economy, and then quickly withdrew American troops from the island in 1906 after restoring order when an insurrection threatened to destroy Cuba's fragile democracy.

Similarly, in the Philippines he stamped out the uprising that had begun after the United States took control of the islands in 1898 and thereby paved the way for the country to eventually become independent after World War II. Though William Jennings Bryan and others on the left called for an immediate American withdrawal from the Philippines, Roosevelt saw that the islands were vulnerable to Japanese or German annexation (the Germans were on the prowl for Pacific colonies) and he wanted to keep the Filipinos under America's wing until they were strong enough to defend themselves. Roosevelt also enacted major land reform in the Philippines, persuading the Catholic Church to sell much of the real estate it owned, which was then parceled out to farmers. He tried to lower the tariff barrier to Filipino imports, but he was barely able to help Cuba in this respect. Given the political opposition in Congress to the idea, he decided not to press his good fortune.

Another area of Roosevelt's foreign policy that is little known is that he was a friend of the Jewish people. After a horrific pogrom within the Russian empire at Kishinev shocked the world, he delivered a petition from American citizens protesting the massacre of Russian Jews (though unlike previous administrations, he did not accompany the petition with an official protest to the Russian government because he believed publicly condemning the Czar was counterproductive). At the end of his life, he embraced the Zionist movement and supported the creation of a Jewish state in Palestine.

RANKING PRESIDENT ROOSEVELT

Despite some marked failures, Theodore Roosevelt ranks among the top tier of American presidents. In fact, in 2010, a Siena University poll of historians placed Theodore Roosevelt as America's second-best president, ahead of Washington and Lincoln, and behind only FDR. Over the last seventy years, polls of historians have consistently put TR among America's top seven presidents.

	Historian Ranking of TR's Presidency
Life magazine (1948)	Seventh
New York Times (1962)	Seventh
Chicago Tribune (1982)	Fourth
New York Times (1994)	Seventh
Wall Street Journal (2000)	Fifth
Average Rank	**Sixth**

Based on the average sixth ranking, Roosevelt was, according to the consensus of historians, a stronger president than nearly 90 percent of those who have led the United States (he surpasses thirty-seven out of forty-two men in the rankings). This pushes him below Abraham Lincoln, George Washington, and Franklin Roosevelt (they occupy the "great" category) and into a second tier of "near greats" that includes Thomas Jefferson, Andrew Jackson, and Woodrow Wilson. The most respected ranking of U.S. presidents in recent years was conducted by the *Wall Street Journal* in 2000. Its survey results were based on an ideologically balanced sample of 132 prominent professors of history, law, and political science. According to these experts, TR was the fifth-greatest president. Similarly, the American people today have a very high opinion of TR, giving him an 89 percent "favorable" rating in a Rasmussen poll conducted in 2007, with only 4 percent expressing an "unfavorable" opinion.

A good argument could be made that he was a stronger president than Jefferson (whose weak management of foreign affairs led directly to the War of 1812) and Jackson (who corrupted American politics with the "spoils system" and did lasting damage to the economy by eliminating the nation's central bank). Wilson has his admirers, but Roosevelt was far more gifted in foreign policy than Wilson, whose presidency effectively ended with his failure to win Senate approval of the severely flawed Versailles Treaty.

A close runner-up to Theodore Roosevelt in achievement might be Ronald Reagan, whose reputation continues to grow. TR and Reagan were optimists who helped raise the spirits of the American people. They were great communicators. They believed in "peace through strength." They believed in American exceptionalism. They shared a love of the outdoors and of the image of the American cowboy. TR laid the groundwork for the American Century and Reagan won the Cold War. Both did much to make a prosperous, strong, confident America. They easily rank as among the most successful conservative politicians in American history, preeminent conservative crusaders.

CHAPTER TWENTY-ONE

FOUNDING FATHER OF THE AMERICAN CENTURY

~

Assessing the presidency of Theodore Roosevelt requires more than grading the success or failure of his specific policies, foreign and domestic. His two terms must be viewed within the arc of American history. The youngest man ever elevated to the White House, he represented a dramatic departure from his presidential predecessors—with the exception of Lincoln—who deferred to Congress, accepting it as the primary branch of government. Roosevelt, in contrast, deferred to no one except the American people, whose tribune he believed he was. Leveraging his magnetic personality and flair for theatrics, he both gave voice to and led a movement of patriotic nationalism and conservative reform. When Roosevelt was thrust into the White House after the assassination of William McKinley, he cast himself as the people's champion—and he delivered—while leaving socialists, populists, and anti-imperialists politically defeated.

Theodore Roosevelt is often labeled a "progressive"—and as far as that means "reformer" it is true. But one cannot understand Theodore

Roosevelt or his politics unless one also recognizes his innate conservatism, which helps explain his adamantine support for the gold standard (he did not pursue currency reform or the creation of a national bank), his moderate trust-busting (it evolved into a policy of utility-like corporate regulation), his refusal to advance tariff reform (notwithstanding his proposal to create a tariff commission), his choice of successor as president (the extremely conservative William Howard Taft), or the politics of his children (very definitely right of center, his eldest son Theodore and FDR campaigned against each other). TR's rhetoric could sometimes sound radical, but it was a radicalism meant to defeat the real radicals; and his record as an elected official was always as a conservative reformer. As president, despite his "progressive" reputation, he pushed only a few major laws through Congress, most of which are forgotten (the one he is remembered for—the Meat Inspection Act—is memorable because of its association with Upton Sinclair's novel, *The Jungle*). His influence on American life was less legislative than it was moral, a call to his fellow Americans to pursue virtue and "the strenuous life."

The *New York Times* captured this salient characteristic of his presidency, writing as he left office:

> It has been the distinguishing merit of Mr. Roosevelt's administration, its most conspicuous achievement, that, seizing upon a propitious moment when scandalous exposures stirred the public resentment against corruption and chicane, he gave the American people a moral shaking up, and with boundless energy, unflagging zeal, and rivers of utterance raised and swelled the tide of their anger until, by punishment actually inflicted or through the deterrent fear of it, hosts of wrongdoers have been driven into honest ways, old abuses stamped out, and a sounder and fair standard of conduct set up.[1]

While TR gave America a moral shaking up, he also broadened its vision. As one pundit observed at the end of TR's administration: "Alexander Hamilton was said to be the first American who could think continentally, Theodore Roosevelt may well be said to be the first of our Presidents who could think internationally."[2]

When Woodrow Wilson declared war against Germany in 1917, his task was made easier, ironically, by the way his arch-nemesis Theodore Roosevelt had prepared the American people for world leadership in general and for entry in this war in particular. In the same way, the heavy blow TR struck against the nation's isolationist tradition helped FDR a generation later when he made the case that the United States should help Britain fight against Nazi Germany.

Given the way his groundbreaking approach to domestic and foreign policy continues to shape the present, we can say without any equivocation that TR was a "founding father" of "the American Century," the man who prepared America to flourish in the modern age, the conservative crusader whose record of statesmanship should be a model for future American presidents.

ACKNOWLEDGMENTS

~

To those who helped make *Theodore the Great: Conservative Crusader* a reality and supported my work along the way, I extend sincere thanks—especially to Alex Novak, Harry Crocker, and the brain trust at Regnery for publishing a book that comes to the defense of a much-maligned American hero. My editor, Bob Patterson, did a masterful job improving the readability of the manuscript; for this valuable contribution and for his keen insights into TR's value system and character, I am very grateful. To Lauren Mann, who did a great job copy editing the book, I say the same.

I am just as appreciative of the contribution made by my literary agent Joan Raines; simply put, without her this book would not exist. I would also like to thank those who provided valuable feedback on the manuscript, including Sharon Kilzer (for making me rethink some of my conclusions), Harry Lembeck (for his insights into TR's race-related attitudes and actions), Jack Caravelli (for his expert take on TR's foreign policy), Robert Morton (for his journalistic perspective on the book) and

Liam Stephens (for helping me understand how the millennial generation sees TR).

My cousin Frank Ruddy, the U.S. Ambassador to Equatorial Guinea during Reagan's presidency, passed away in 2014; I mourn his loss and must acknowledge his contribution to this book. Many years ago over dinner at the Cosmos Club in Washington he revealed to me his antipathy for TR, branding our "Square Deal" president a "self-serving demagogue" for his "war on the rich" (the topic came up because TR is one of the club's most famous members and we were sitting under his portrait as we ate). It was the first time I realized how much dyed-in-the-wool conservatives like Frank disliked TR. This discovery piqued my interest in learning whether their negative view of him was fair and that curiosity ultimately led to this book. It is too bad Frank is no longer with us as I would relish the chance to persuade him with a gift copy of my book that TR wasn't so bad after all.

Words are not sufficient to describe my gratitude to Edmund Morris, whose empathy and counsel at a pivotal moment made all the difference in the world; the height of his generosity is rivaled only by his literary greatness.

A large contingent of my family helped in ways too numerous to list. They include my sisters Marianne Ruddy-Pinto, Lainie Ruddy-Davanzo, Sheila Ruddy-Heerdt, Laurie Ruddy-Hoffman, Jeanne Ruddy-Gutches and Deirdre Ruddy; and my brothers Chris Ruddy, Peter Ruddy and Tom Ruddy. My warm thanks also go out to Carolyn McNitt, whose unwavering loyalty and tireless encouragement over many years has been a brisk wind filling my creative sails. To everyone who helped me and to that mysterious spiritual agency that is essential to any creative process, what Shakespeare called the "muse of fire" that ascends "the brightest heaven of invention," I am deeply grateful.

GUIDE TO

SOURCES

~

To offer a fresh interpretation of Theodore Roosevelt and avoid a mere regurgitation of the writings of other historians, this book is almost entirely based on primary source material, supplemented by contemporary newspaper accounts that appeared during his life. The canon of Roosevelt scholarship that has been amassed over the last century was used to fact check the text of the manuscript, ensure important issues were not overlooked, and provide insights and citations as needed. In constructing the book this way, I have consciously adopted the method of historian James Thomas Flexner, whose multivolume biography of George Washington represents a literary monument of fair, thorough, and original scholarship.

PRIMARY SOURCES

During his incredibly active career, Roosevelt amassed a voluminous paper record, which is contained in four main depositories (see below).

Those who tap into this indispensable primary-source material can literally hear him speak his mind (most of the 150,000 letters he generated during his life were dictated to a stenographer). The research of this book was laid through a lengthy, on-and-off examination of this endlessly interesting log of his day-to-day life, a learning process that began in 2007 with the research for my first book, *Theodore Roosevelt's History of the United States*, and ended when I sat down to write this book in 2014.

Works   *The Works of Theodore Roosevelt.* Edited by Herman Hagedorn, National Edition, 20 vols. New York: Scribner's, 1926. Includes all of TR's books, and most of his essays and speeches.

Letters   *The Letters of Theodore Roosevelt.* 8 vols. Edited by Elting Morison and John Blum. Cambridge, MA: Harvard University Press, 1951–1954. The most interesting TR letters (including those in the Theodore Roosevelt Papers held in the Library of Congress) are published in these eight volumes.

Papers   *Theodore Roosevelt Papers.* Washington, DC: Library of Congress, 485 reels of microfilm containing letters to and from TR, mostly after 1897. Nearly all of these TR letters were dictated to a stenographer, and are copies of originals sent to recipients.

Collection *Theodore Roosevelt Collection.* Cambridge, MA: Harvard College Library. Main manuscript source of pre-1897 TR material, and main repository for family letters before and after. This collection also includes a massive amount of other TR-related material.

NEWSPAPER RECORDS

"Newspapers," as the saying goes, "are the first draft of history." They are often neglected by historians; the information they provide is sometimes inaccurate and almost always incomplete. They also contain an enormous amount of extraneous information that makes it a difficult task to find the "good stuff"—the nuggets of colorful detail that bring a book to life. For example, imagine having to wade through forty years' worth of the *New York Times* between 1880 and 1920 to learn all this newspaper had to say about Roosevelt (that's fifteen-thousand days worth of material!). In the past, it was impossible for historians to read through so much verbiage from a single newspaper, let alone from more than one.

With the creation of digital databases during the past fifteen years, however, immense archives have now been opened up to wider use. Instead of reading through an entire newspaper archive, a historian can now do a keyword search to find topics he or she is looking for. Thus, if one wants to see every reference to TR and Bismarck between 1880 and 2000 (over a century's worth of time), one can access those stories instantly. Leveraging this new research tool with its magical ability to unearth hidden gems, I extracted a large amount of information about TR that has until now never been accessible. As part of my research, I downloaded roughly four thousand articles from the digital databases of the following newspapers, which are abbreviated in the notes as follows:

AC	*Atlanta Constitution*
BG	*Boston Globe*
BS	*Baltimore Sun*
CE	*Cincinnati Enquirer*
CT	*Chicago Tribune*
DFP	*Detroit Free Press*
HC	*Hartford Courant*
LAT	*Los Angeles Times*
LT	*London Times*

NYT	*New York Times*
SFC	*San Francisco Chronicle*
SPD	*St. Louis Post-Dispatch*
ST	*Sunday Times of London*
WP	*Washington Post*

PUBLISHED WORKS AND NON-TR MANUSCRIPT ARCHIVES

It was impossible to read through the eight hundred books written about Roosevelt over the last century; the most important ones were consulted as part of the research for this book. Personal letters and newspaper accounts have their deficiencies as source material (one is heavily biased in TR's favor; the other is notoriously incomplete). Published books about his life have weaknesses, too; they tend to parrot other historians, creating an inbred narrative that perpetuates myths and biases, and in the end fails to flesh out his character in a new way. To avoid this danger, researchers must at times free themselves from the "historical consensus" and strike out on their own by diving head first into the primary sources.

My exploration of the four main depositories of TR's papers was extended into hit-or-miss investigations of a handful of manuscript archives of his most important advisors (like Henry Cabot Lodge) and uniquely placed eyewitnesses (like his military aide Archie Butt). These journeys into neglected primary-source material have yielded some rich insights but unfortunately could not be exploited in full measure due to time constraints.

Beale   Beale, Howard. *Theodore Roosevelt and the Rise of America to World Power*. Baltimore: Johns Hopkins Press, 1956.

Bishop

Bishop, Joseph Bucklin. *Theodore Roosevelt and his Time.* 2 vols. New York: Scribner's, 1920. Extensive excerpts from TR's letters, many of which can also be found in the *Letters, Papers,* and *Collection.*

Blum

Blum, John. *The Republican Roosevelt.* Cambridge, MA: Harvard University Press, 1965. Written in an opaque academic style that is nearly impenetrable and thus not recommended for average readers.

Bowman

Bowman, Isaiah. *Isaiah Bowman Papers.* Baltimore: Johns Hopkins University. Contains a monograph account of Bowman's visit to Sagamore Hill in 1915, in which he vividly describes the ex-president.

Brinkley

Brinkley, Douglas. *The Wilderness Warrior.* New York: Harper Perennial, 2010. The definitive account of TR's conservation record.

Butt

Butt, Archie. *The Letters of Archie Butt: Personal Aide to President Roosevelt.* Edited by Lawrence Abbott. New York: Doubleday, Page & Company, 1924. One of the best eyewitness accounts of TR from his gossipy military aide, Archie Butt, who died in 1912 as a passenger aboard the *Titanic.*

Butt Papers   *Archibald Butt Papers*. Morrow, GA: Georgia
                           Archives. Contains the complete, unedited ver-
                           sions of the Butt Letters published in 1924.
                           Some of the juiciest material was cut out of the
                           published letters.

Churchill   Churchill, Allen. *The Roosevelts: American
                           Aristocrats*. New York: Harper & Row, 1965.

Clowes   "The War with the United States, 1812–1815,"
                           by Theodore Roosevelt (in William Laird
                           Clowes, *The Royal Navy*, 6: 1–180, London:
                           Sampson Low, 1901). An abridged, reworked
                           version of TR's book, *The Naval War of 1812*.

Cutright   Cutright, Paul Russell. *Theodore Roosevelt:
                           The Making of a Conservationist*. Champaign,
                           IL: University of Illinois Press, 1985. A well-
                           researched account of TR's crusade to preserve
                           the nation's natural resources.

Dalton   Dalton, Kathleen. *Theodore Roosevelt: A
                           Strenuous Life*. New York: Alfred A. Knopf,
                           2002. A leftist interpretation of TR's life,
                           focusing on his progressive achievements.

Decoppett   Decoppett, Andre. *Andre Decoppett Collec-
                           tion*, Manuscripts Division, Department of
                           Rare Books & Special Collections, Princeton
                           University Library. A collection that includes
                           a handful of TR's letters.

Dodd Papers   Dodd, William E. *William E. Dodd Papers.* Washington, DC: Library of Congress. Contains an interesting account of Dodd's lunch with TR at the White House.

Hagedorn   Hagedorn, Hermann. *The Roosevelt Family of Sagamore Hill.* New York: Macmillan Company, 1954.

Hale   Hale, William Bayard. *A Week in The White House With Theodore Roosevelt.* New York: G. P. Putnam's Sons, 1908.

Harbaugh   Harbaugh, William. *The Life and Times of Theodore Roosevelt.* New York: Farrar, Strauss and Cudahy, 1961. Written in the somewhat dry prose of the academy, but a solid factual account of TR's career.

Hath   Huth, Hans. *Nature and the American.* Lincoln, NE: University of Nebraska Press, 1957.

Jay Papers   *Jay Family Papers.* Columbia University Library. A manuscript collection that includes TR's letters to John Jay, a friend of TR's father.

Kearns   Kearns Goodwin, Doris. *The Bully Pulpit: Theodore Roosevelt, William Howard Taft, and the Golden Age of Journalism.* New York: Simon & Schuster, 2014.

Leary

Leary, John J. Jr. *Talks with T.R.* Boston: Houghton Mifflin Company, 1920. Remembrances of one of TR's journalist friends.

Lodge Letters

Lodge, Henry Cabot. *Selections from the Correspondence of Theodore Roosevelt and Henry Cabot Lodge.* New York: Scribner's, 1925. The complete, unedited collection of TR-HCL letters can be found in the Lodge Papers.

Lodge Papers

Lodge, Henry Cabot. *Henry Cabot Lodge Papers.* Boston: Massachusetts Historical Society.

Matthews

Matthews, Brander. *An Introduction to The Study of American Literature.* 1896.

McCullough

McCullough, David. *Mornings on Horseback.* New York: Simon & Schuster, 1981. A narrative account of TR's early life, with an emphasis on the lives of his parents, siblings, and extended family, explaining how those closest to him shaped his character.

Morris Rise

Morris, Edmund. *The Rise of Theodore Roosevelt.* New York: Coward, McCann & Geoghegan, 1979. I owe a large personal debt to this book, one of the greatest nonfiction works of the twentieth century. It was the first book I read about TR, beginning the journey that has culminated in this book.

Morris Rex   Morris, Edmund. *Theodore Rex*. New York: Random House, 2001. The best narrative account of TR's presidency. This book is underappreciated because of the luminescence of Morris's *The Rise of Theodore Roosevelt*.

Morris Colonel   Morris, Edmund. *Colonel Roosevelt*. New York: Random House, 2010. In some ways the most impressive of Morris's trilogy in the way it overcomes the melancholy subject matter, which of necessity deals with the decline of a great man.

Morris Eleanor   Morris, Sylvia Jukes. *Edith Kermit Roosevelt*. New York: Coward, McCann and Geoghegan, 1980.

Morse Papers   Morse, John Torrey. *John Torrey Morse Papers*. Boston: Massachusetts Historical Society. Henry Cabot Lodge's cousin and the editor of TR's biographies of Gouverneur Morris and Thomas Hart Benton.

Presidential Addresses   *Presidential Addresses and State Papers of Theodore Roosevelt*. New York: P. F. Collier & Son. 4 vols. Kraus Reprint Co., 1970.

Pringle　　Pringle, Henry. *Theodore Roosevelt: A Biography*. New York: Harcourt, Brace & Co., 1931 [foreword written by Pringle added in 1956 edition]. A persuasive critique of TR, but its portrayal of him as a "magnificent child" is unfair. With only three paragraphs devoted to conservation and reclamation (two of TR's greatest achievements), the book contains some glaring omissions that undermine its credibility, yet nonetheless remains one of the best books about him.

Putnam　　Putnam, Carleton. *Theodore Roosevelt: The Formative Years, 1858–1886*. New York: Scribner's, 1958. A wonderful account of TR's early life that makes one wish the author had written additional volumes.

Rhodes Papers　　Rhodes, James Ford. *James Ford Rhodes Papers*. Boston: Massachusetts Historical Society. Rhodes was one of TR's favorite historians and well connected politically, his sister being married to Mark Hanna.

Rhodes　　Rhodes, James Ford. *The McKinley and Roosevelt Administrations, 1897–1909*. New York: Macmillan, 1923.

Wagenknecht　　Wagenknecht, Edward. *The Seven Worlds of Theodore Roosevelt*. London: Longmans, Green & Co., 1958. A vividly detailed description of TR's multi-faceted character.

Vidal

Vidal, Gore. *Empire*. New York: Random House, 1987. An interesting take on TR in the context of a historical novel, which portrays him as a ruthless politician and the moral equivalent of William Randolph Hearst.

NOTES

EPIGRAPHS AND INTRODUCTION

1. LT, September 3, 1910.
2. Works, 13: 44.
3. Pringle, 365.
4. NYT, January 6, 1929.
5. BG, January 27, 1919.
6. BG, January 27, 1919.
7. Works, 10: 190.
8. LT, April 12, 1932.
9. Works, 7: 427.
10. Works, 16: 91.
11. "Socialism," Outlook, March 20, 1909.
12. CE, June 6, 1918.

CHAPTER ONE: TR'S ROLLER-COASTER REPUTATION

1. LT, April 13, 1907.

2. BS, February 7, 1909; February 14, 1909.

3. One of TR's now forgotten crusades was for simplified spelling.

4. NYT, September 20, 1896.

5. Letters, TR to W. White, December 12, 1910.

6. Letters, TR to A. Lee, June 17, 1915.

7. BG, October 21, 1979.

8. Pringle, vii.

9. Pringle, 75.

10. CT, June 4, 1961.

11. WP, November 12, 1938.

12. CT, June 4, 1961.

13. Morris Rex, 9.

14. Letters, TR to A. Scott, June 26, 1907.

15. Letters, TR to HCL, December 6, 1898.

CHAPTER TWO: DELIGHTED DEFENDER OF FAMILY AND COUNTRY

1. Morris Colonel, 198.

2. WP, March 12, 1897.

3. NYT, October 22, 1933.

4. LT, December 9, 1915.

5. Lodge Papers, TR to HCL, February 15, 1887.

6. Lodge Papers, TR to HCL, October 20, 1899.

7. Lodge Papers, TR to HCL, July 11, 1889.

8. Lodge Papers, TR to HCL, September 27, 1889.

9. Pringle, 40.

10. Letters, TR to A. Lee, August 1, 1914.

11. Morris Rise, 24.

12. Lodge Letters, TR to HCL, July 4, 1893.

13. Papers, TR to H. Otis, August 5, 1903.

14. Letters, TR to L. Abbott, July 26, 1904.

15. Works, 14: 43.

16. NYT, October 22, 1933.

17. BS, September 21, 1903.

18. Pringle, 4.
19. Pringle, 345.
20. Morris Colonel, 115
21. LT, May 16, 1910.
22. Pringle, 417.
23. NYT, February 25, 1936.
24. Letters, TR to G. Aiton, May 15, 1901.
25. LAT, June 29, 1895.
26. NYT, July 21, 1895.
27. NYT, April 23, 1899.
28. LT, August 10, 1899.
29. LT, October 15, 1901.
30. LT, September 16, 1901.
31. BS, May 15, 1902.
32. Dodd Papers, Memorandum, March 5, 1908.
33. Works, 7: 422.
34. Works, 7: 26.
35. BS, September 21, 1903.
36. SPD, January 1, 1909.
37. SPD, January 1, 1909.
38. WP, October 29, 1896.
39. NYT, November 14, 1906.
40. NYT, June 31, 1921.
41. BS, December 14, 1907.
42. William Howard Taft Presidential Papers, W. Taft to his wife, March 31, 1904.
43. Leary, 178.
44. Pringle, 65.
45. Papers, TR to E. Forbush, July 21, 1904.
46. Morris Rex, 108.
47. LT, September 16, 1901.
48. Morris Rex, 452.
49. LT, November 9, 1988.
50. NYT, January 19, 1936.

51. TR to W. Reid, April 21, 1906.

52. TR to J. Hay, April 2, 1905.

53. Letters, TR to A. H. Lee, September 4, 1914.

54. Letters, TR to G. Lorimer, May 12, 1906.

55. Works, 7: 458.

56. Works, 13: 172.

57. Works, 13: 172.

58. Vidal, 341.

59. Letters, TR to E. Roosevelt, June 24, 1906.

60. Works, 13: 10.

61. HCL to TR, August 1, 1905.

CHAPTER THREE: MISCONCEPTIONS ABOUT TR

1. Letters, TR to J. Lowell, February 20, 1900.

2. Works, 13: 565.

3. Works, 13: 564–65.

4. Works, 13: 44.

5. Works, 7: 102.

6. LT, December 9, 1903.

7. BG, April 18, 1961.

8. CT, September 2, 1901.

9. Letters, TR to ARC, May 15, 1886.

10. LT, March 23, 1906.

11. LT, September 23, 1916.

12. Morris Rex, 310.

13. Morris Rex, 458.

14. Works, 12: 283–84.

15. Works, 12: 284.

16. William Howard Taft Presidential Papers, W. Taft to E. Parker, November 16, 1914.

17. LT, May 6, 1910.

18. NYT, April 15, 1907.

19. Morris Rex, 486.

CHAPTER FOUR: THE BULL MOOSE PROGRESSIVE

1. Harbaugh, 361.
2. NYT, May 6, 1910.
3. NYT, August 8, 1912.
4. LT, February 26, 1912.
5. LT, April 27, 1912.
6. LT, April 27, 1912.
7. CT, February 27, 1912.
8. Letters, TR to HCL, September 9, 1913.
9. Letters, TR to W. White, May 28, 1917.
10. Woodrow Wilson to TR, July 28, 1901.
11. Letters, TR to C. Dodge, June 16, 1902.
12. BS, June 12, 1913.
13. NYT, October 4, 1913.
14. Letters, TR to HCL, September 9, 1913.
15. Letters, TR to K. Roosevelt, August 28, 1915.

CHAPTER FIVE: TR'S POLITICAL EDUCATION

1. LT, September 19, 1901.
2. NYT, March 18, 1885.
3. CT, March 6, 1883.
4. AC, February 22, 1885.
5. CT, July 21, 1884.
6. DFP, August 3, 1889.
7. WP, August 3, 1889.
8. NYT, May 29, 1883.
9. NYT, October 16, 1886.
10. CT, November 25, 1890.
11. The Outlook, "William H. Taft: An Appreciation," by Lyman Abbott, April 4, 1908.
12. Letters, TR to HCL, June 29, 1889.
13. Lodge Papers, TR to HCL, July 1, 1891.
14. Lodge Papers, TR to HCL, October 31, 1890.
15. Lodge Papers, TR to HCL, July 22, 1891.
16. Lodge Papers, TR to HCL, October 4, 1890.

17. Pringle, 86.
18. NYT, April 25, 1895.
19. WP, July 17, 1895.
20. BG, January 27, 1919.

CHAPTER SIX: TR'S RUN-UP TO THE WHITE HOUSE

1. TR to S. Diblee, February 16, 1898.
2. BS, November 5, 1898.
3. NYT, March 28, 1899.
4. NYT, April 29, 1899.
5. HC, May 1, 1899.
6. Letters, TR to L. Wood, April 17, 1901.
7. Letters, TR to T. Platt, November 27, 1899.
8. WP, June 20, 1900.
9. BS, April 13, 1900.
10. NYT, October 17, 1931.

CHAPTER SEVEN: THE TRUST-BUSTER MYTH

1. LT, November 4, 1886.
2. Collection, TR to ARC, September 27, 1896.
3. TR to H. Kohlsaat, August 7, 1899.
4. CT, January 4, 1900.
5. CT, January 4, 1900.
6. CT, January 4, 1900.
7. NYT, January 4, 1900.
8. LAT, April 5, 1901.
9. Morris Rex, 60.
10. BG, February 21, 1902.
11. BG, February 21, 1902.
12. CT, June 6, 1902.
13. NYT, July 15, 1902.
14. NYT, June 24, 1904.
15. SPD, September 23, 1902.
16. TR to W. Le Gendre, August 13, 1903.
17. TR to R. Collier, October 19, 1902.

18. SPD, March 15, 1904.

19. SPD, October 21, 1904.

20. NYT, January 8, 1909.

21. CT, January 14, 1909.

CHAPTER EIGHT: SIDESTEPPING THE TARIFF THIRD RAIL

1. LT, May 3, 1909.

2. Letters, TR to R. Bowker, October 31, 1884.

3. DFP, June 2, 1883.

4. SFC, October 20, 1886.

5. Lodge Letters, 2: 121.

6. Harbaugh, 360.

7. Letters, TR to N. Butler, August 12, 1902.

8. TR to Unknown, January 21, 1915.

9. ST, August 6, 1899.

CHAPTER NINE: NEGLECTING CURRENCY/ BANKING REFORM

1. LT, December 3, 1902.

2. Works, 7: 89–90.

3. Letters, TR to H. White, November 27, 1907.

CHAPTER TEN: SETTING THE MODEL FOR LABOR DISPUTES

1. Letters, TR to B. Wheeler, June 17, 1908.

2. NYT, August 30, 1902.

3. NYT, October 2, 1902.

4. NYT, October 3, 1902.

5. LT, October 17, 1902.

6. NYT, November 18, 1941.

CHAPTER ELEVEN: PROTECTING CONSUMER HEALTH AND SAFETY

1. CT, March 3, 1907.

2. LT, May 29, 1906.

3. BG, June 5, 1906.

4. BG, June 5, 1906.

5. NYT, June 30, 1906.

CHAPTER TWELVE: CONSERVING NATURAL RESOURCES

1. Cutright, 216.

2. Cutright, 216.

3. Cutright, 238.

4. Cutright, 238.

5. Huth, *Journal of the Warburg and Courtlauld Institutes*, Vol. 13, 1950.

6. Cutright, 177.

7. Cutright, 178.

8. Cutright, 206.

9. Cutright, 173.

10. Cutright, 184.

11. Cutright, 204.

12. NYT, April 15, 1907.

13. NYT, May 7, 1903.

14. Cutright, 218.

15. Cutright, 223.

CHAPTER THIRTEEN: DELIVERING WATER TO THE ARID WEST

1. Papers, TR to G. Chamberlain, May 7, 1907.

2. CT, July 11, 1886.

3. BG, September 21, 1904.

4. Morris Rex, 21.

5. BG, April 18, 1961.

6. NYT, March 17, 1985.

7. Morris Rex, 115.

CHAPTER FOURTEEN: WINNING—THEN LOSING— BLACK VOTERS

1. Letters, TR to H. Pritchett, December 14, 1904.

2. TR to J. Bishop, February 17, 1903.

3. Rhodes Papers, Index Rerum, November 16, 1905.

4. Letters, TR to O. Wister, April 27, 1906.

5. Letters, TR to J. Harris, August 1, 1912.

6. Works, 9: 44–45.

7. Letters, TR to O. Wister, April 27, 1906.

8. BS, October 19, 1900.

9. WP, March 5, 1901.

10. WP, March 5, 1901.

11. SPD, October 18, 1901.

12. SPD, October 24, 1901.

13. Letters, TR to O. Wister, April 27, 1906.

14. Letters, TR to HCL, June 29, 1889.

15. Letters, TR to A. Tourgee, November 8, 1901.

16. Harbaugh, 291.

17. Letters, TR to H. Pritchett, December 14, 1904.

18. LS, December 24, 1970.

19. NYT, November 19, 1906.

CHAPTER FIFTEEN: BRITAIN: FORGING THE SPECIAL RELATIONSHIP

1. Collection, The Market World, April 1908, 8.

2. HC, November 22, 1886.

3. HC, November 22, 1886.

4. Collection, The Market World, April 1908, 7.

5. Letters, TR to J. Matthews, December 6, 1895.

6. Letters, TR to W. Cowles, December 22, 1895.

7. Letters, TR to F. Selous, February 7, 1900.

8. NYT, November 20, 1901.

9. BS, November 20, 1901.

10. LT, December 17, 1901.

11. LT, June 7, 1910.

12. Letters, TR to B. McCalla, August 3, 1897.

13. TR to C. Spring Rice, March 2, 1900.

14. TR to C. Spring Rice, March 12, 1900.
15. TR to C. Spring Rice, July 3, 1901.
16. LT, March 16, 1903.
17. LT, February 26, 1903.
18. BS, November 6, 1903.
19. LT, December 8, 1903.
20. LT, November 11, 1904.
21. LT, November 19, 1902.
22. LT, January 19, 1909.
23. LT, June 1, 1910.
24. LT, June 2, 1910.
25. TR to G. Putnam, December 8, 1918.

CHAPTER SIXTEEN: GERMANY: RESTRAINING THE KAISER

1. CT, February 13, 1898.
2. Works, 18: 225.
3. TR to C. Moore, February 14, 1898.
4. TR to C. Spring Rice, August 13, 1897.
5. Dalton, 165.
6. LT, December 31, 1901.
7. LT, December 31, 1901.
8. LT, December 31, 1901.
9. NYT, December 16, 1901.
10. LT, December 12, 1902.
11. LT, September 29, 1917.
12. TR to C. Spring Rice, August 13, 1897.
13. TR to G. Trevelyan, October 1, 1911.
14. CT, September 21, 1926.
15. *Prejudices*, Alfred A. Knopf, Chapter 11: "Roosevelt: An Autopsy," by H. L. Mencken.
16. TR to J. Hay, April 2, 1905.
17. TR to W. Taft, April 20, 1905.
18. TR to C. Spring Rice, May 13, 1905.
19. TR to W. Reid, April 21, 1906.

20. TR to W. Reid, April 21, 1906.

21. CT, March 26, 1906.

CHAPTER SEVENTEEN: JAPAN: PREVENTING WAR IN THE PACIFIC

1. Letters, TR to A. Mahan, May 3, 1897.

2. Problem for War College, May 26, 1897.

3. Letters, TR to A. Mahan, May 3, 1897.

4. TR to C. Spring Rice, November 19, 1900.

5. TR to C. Spring Rice, June 13, 1903.

6. TR to C. Spring Rice, November 1, 1905.

7. BS, May 15, 1903.

8. CT, April 25, 1948.

9. LT, May 1, 1905.

10. Letters, TR to E. Hale, October 27, 1906.

11. NYT, October 2, 1938.

12. TR to C. Spring Rice, July 24, 1905.

13. TR to C. Spring Rice, July 24, 1905.

14. TR to G. Meyer, June 19, 1905.

15. LT, October 2, 1905.

16. NYT, February 22, 1916.

17. NYT, March 5, 1916.

18. Harbaugh, 266.

19. TR to H. Von Sternberg, August 28, 1900.

20. Morris Rex, 400.

21. Butt Papers, Butt Letter to his Mother, July 29, 1908.

22. NYT, August 8, 1924.

23. NYT, December 8, 1906.

24. TR to HCL, June 5, 1905.

25. LT, October 26, 1906.

26. SPD, June 6, 1907.

27. NYT, November 5, 1931.

28. Powell, 318.

29. NYT, April 28, 1907.

30. LT, July 9, 1907.

CHAPTER EIGHTEEN: PANAMA: MAKING THE DIRT FLY

1. TR to S. Small, December 29, 1903.
2. LT, September 24, 1903.
3. TR to R. Kipling, November 1, 1904.
4. TR to R. Kipling, November 1, 1904.
5. TR to W. Thayer, July 2, 1915.
6. Letters, TR to A. Shaw, November 6, 1903.
7. BS, June 14, 1903.
8. NYT, November 5, 1903.
9. LT, November 7, 1903.
10. NYT, November 6, 1903.
11. BS, November 6, 1903.
12. NYT, November 6, 1903.
13. NYT, November 5, 1903.
14. Morris Rex, 301.
15. NYT, September 23, 1907.
16. TR to Senate Foreign Affairs Committee, July 11, 1914.

CHAPTER NINETEEN: MONROE DOCTRINE: ADDING A POLICE POWER

1. LT, May 23, 1904.
2. LT, December 31, 1901.
3. Morris Rex, 178.
4. TR to C. Spring Rice, June 13, 1903.
5. LT, January 7, 1913.
6. LT, May 23, 1904.
7. LT, May 25, 1904.
8. BS, April 21, 1907.
9. LT, February 15, 1899.
10. CT, October 3, 1906.

CHAPTER TWENTY: ONE OF THE GREATEST PRESIDENTS

1. Harbaugh, 112.

2.   LT, March 24, 1908.

3.   WP, March 1, 1909.

CHAPTER TWENTY-ONE: FOUNDING FATHER OF THE AMERICAN CENTURY

1.   NYT, March 4, 1909.

2.   WP, March 1, 1909.

INDEX